Aid During Conflict

Interaction Between Military and
Civilian Assistance Providers in
Afghanistan, September 2001–
June 2002

Olga Oliker, Richard Kauzlarich, James Dobbins,
Kurt W. Basseuner, Donald L. Sampler, John G. McGinn,
Michael J. Dziedzic, Adam Grissom, Bruce Pirnie,
Nora Bensahel, A. Istar Guven

Prepared for the Office of the Secretary of Defense
and the U.S. Agency for International Development

 NATIONAL DEFENSE RESEARCH INSTITUTE

The research described in this report was sponsored by the Office of the Secretary of Defense (OSD) and the U.S. Agency for International Development. The research was conducted in the RAND National Defense Research Institute, a federally funded research and development center supported by the OSD, the Joint Staff, the unified commands, and the defense agencies under Contract DASW01-01-C-0004.

Library of Congress Cataloging-in-Publication Data

Aid during conflict : interaction between military and civilian assistance providers in
  Afghanistan, September 2001–June 2002 / Olga Oliker ... [et al.].
    p. cm.
  "MG-212."
  Includes bibliographical references.
  ISBN 0-8330-3640-8 (pbk. : alk. paper)
  1. Afghan War, 2001—Civilian relief. I. Oliker, Olga.

  DS371.415.A36 2004
  958.104'7—dc22

                                                                    2004013220

The RAND Corporation is a nonprofit research organization providing objective analysis and effective solutions that address the challenges facing the public and private sectors around the world. RAND's publications do not necessarily reflect the opinions of its research clients and sponsors.

RAND® is a registered trademark.

Published 2004 by the RAND Corporation
1700 Main Street, P.O. Box 2138, Santa Monica, CA 90407-2138
1200 South Hayes Street, Arlington, VA 22202-5050
201 North Craig Street, Suite 202, Pittsburgh, PA 15213-1516
RAND URL: http://www.rand.org/
To order RAND documents or to obtain additional information, contact
Distribution Services: Telephone: (310) 451-7002;
Fax: (310) 451-6915; Email: order@rand.org

Preface

The Afghanistan experience may eventually be seen as a turning point for U.S. government involvement in the provision of humanitarian and humanitarian-type assistance in complex operations like Operation Enduring Freedom (OEF). From the perspectives of both military and civilian assistance providers, the first year in Afghanistan was generally successful. A major humanitarian disaster was averted, refugee flows were handled effectively, and assistance helped stabilize the country. At the same time, the first eight months of OEF highlighted coordination challenges among the various military and civilian personnel providing such assistance in Afghanistan. Some aspects of OEF, such as the continuation of major combat operations while reconstruction and state-building activities were ongoing, were unique, and even potentially precedent-setting. Other aspects, such as tension between military and civilian assistance providers over proper roles, were familiar from past operations.

This report assesses relief, reconstruction, humanitarian, and humanitarian-type aid efforts in Afghanistan from October 2001 to June 2002. It also evaluates coordination among various civilian and military aid providers and concludes with a list of recommendations for government policymakers, implementers, and civilian aid providers.

This research involved a variety of sources and methods. It began with a two-day conference (October 7–8, 2002), which brought together representatives of a broad range of civilian and military assistance providers, individuals familiar with both civil-military issues in general and those peculiar to this situation, to discuss the Afghanistan experience. Participants included representatives from the policy offices of the Pentagon, various nongovernmental organizations (NGOs), the United Nations, Britain's Department for International Development (DFID), the U.S. Agency for International Development (USAID), and other U.S. government agencies. The conference provided a critical starting point, sharpening and defining the study. The research team then gathered written materials on assistance generally and assistance in Afghanistan specifically and conducted a series of in-depth interviews with military personnel, U.S. government officials, and representatives of NGOs and international organizations (IOs) involved in providing assistance. These interviews took place both in the United States and in Afghanistan.

The study reported here was a joint research effort conducted for USAID and the Office of the Assistant Secretary of Defense for Special Operations and Low Intensity Conflict. It was carried out within the United States Institute of Peace (USIP) and the RAND Corporation's National Defense Research Institute.

RAND's National Defense Research Institute is a federally funded research and development center sponsored by the Office of the Secretary of Defense, the Joint Staff, the unified commands, and the defense agencies. For more information on RAND's National Defense Research Institute, contact Acting Director Gene Gritton. He can be reached by e-mail at Gene_Gritton@rand.org; by phone at 310-393-0411, extension 6933; or by mail at RAND, 1700 Main Street, Santa Monica, California 90407-2138. More information about RAND is available at www.rand.org.

USIP was created in 1984 by the U.S. Congress as an independent, nonpartisan federal institution to promote the prevention, management, and peaceful resolution of international conflicts. USIP is well known and widely respected for its broad range of research programs, in particular its work on civil-military relations in post-conflict situations.

This study somewhat emphasizes the military aspect of civil-military operations in Afghanistan, since the period covered (September 2001 to June 2002) was the most intense phase of military operations. It therefore should be of particular interest to defense and foreign-policy decisionmakers, practitioners, and analysts. Despite the military emphasis, however, the analysis and recommendations herein should also interest the broad humanitarian assistance community and those concerned with relief and development assistance in conflict and post-conflict situations. Comments are welcome and should be addressed to the study's authors.

The RAND Corporation Quality Assurance Process

Peer review is an integral part of all RAND research projects. Prior to publication, this document, as with all documents in the RAND monograph series, was subject to a quality assurance process to ensure that the research meets several standards, including the following: The problem is well formulated; the research approach is well designed and well executed; the data and assumptions are sound; the findings are useful and advance knowledge; the implications and recommendations follow logically from the findings and are explained thoroughly; the documentation is accurate, understandable, cogent, and temperate in tone; the research demonstrates understanding of related previous studies; and the research is relevant, objective, independent, and balanced. Peer review is conducted by research professionals who were not members of the project team.

RAND routinely reviews and refines its quality assurance process and also conducts periodic external and internal reviews of the quality of its body of work. For additional details regarding the RAND quality assurance process, visit

http://www.rand.org/standards/.

Contents

Summary

International assistance efforts in Afghanistan were broadly successful during the initial stages of Operation Enduring Freedom (OEF), from September 2001 to June 2002. A major humanitarian catastrophe was averted by the hard work of many actors, governmental and nongovernmental, civilian and military. The early Afghanistan experience also involved problems and challenges, however, which may be seen as lessons for future operations.

Critical Issues

In some ways, humanitarian and humanitarian-type assistance operations in Afghanistan were unlike any in the past. Lack of an international peacekeeping mandate beyond the city of Kabul, a tightly limited in-country military footprint, and security-dictated restrictions on movement of U.S. government (USG) civilians were important new features. Since the initial period of OEF was the most intense phase of military operations, this report focuses primarily on the military aspects of civil-military operations (CMOs) in Afghanistan. Some of the critical issues, both positive and negative, identified by this study are summarized below.

Strategic Level

- The absence of an integrated interagency political-military plan from the early stages of the campaign contributed to confusion about roles and missions.
- There was extended uncertainty regarding whether U.S. military humanitarian-type assistance activities would be "wholesale" (limited to logistics outside Afghanistan) or "retail" (also including direct provision and coordination activities inside Afghanistan).
- Coordination between the U.S. Agency for International Development (USAID) and the Department of Defense (DoD) was good.
- Liaison between U.S. Central Command (CENTCOM) and nongovernmental organizations (NGOs) and international organizations (IOs), including the United Nations (UN) specialized agencies, proved useful.

Field Level

- There were difficulties in establishing effective CMO coordination bodies and requesting and deploying civil-affairs units.
- Operational-level coordination between military personnel and NGOs and IOs was often poor.
- Differing views of the role of the U.S. military in providing humanitarian-type assistance and of appropriate terminology contributed to tensions between military personnel and civilian assistance providers from contractors, NGOs, and UN agencies. Particular tensions emerged over the forms of assistance provided and the question of whether military personnel should wear uniforms when providing assistance.
- USAID personnel were unable to travel to unsecured areas and had difficulty accessing project funds quickly.

Given the immense time pressures, an unsettled international environment following 9/11, and new challenges stemming from the

USG's status as a "belligerent" in the eyes of some actors, it is perhaps surprising that CMOs were as successful as they were in Afghanistan. While some challenges were unique to the Afghan campaign, others are likely to be repeated. In addition, some problems experienced in earlier operations emerged here as well.

Recommendations

USG Civil-Military Operations

- **Conduct early political-military planning.** An integrated political-military planning process should precede future interventions and should explicitly incorporate the role of humanitarian-type assistance in achieving the military and political end-states:

  - Clearly define and communicate USG policy within the USG and to other assistance providers.
  - Establish clear CMO chains of command. Decisionmakers should consider naming a single person as the coordinator for all in-theater USG agency assistance programs.
  - Institutionalize mechanisms for transitioning from military to nonmilitary humanitarian and humanitarian-type assistance processes.

- **Conduct joint political-military planning.** There is a need for better integration of USAID, the State Department, and DoD in developing and implementing the overall political-military plan. Decisionmakers should consider a Federal Emergency Management Agency (FEMA)–type structure to plan and coordinate USG humanitarian-type assistance.
- **Provide security for humanitarian assistance and reconstruction.** It is important for the USG to develop an integrated capacity—civilian, military, and international—to establish public security in the aftermath of high-intensity conflict. U.S. military forces should not be expected to shoulder these burdens single-handedly, but neither, in many cases, can indigenous forces,

civil agencies, and international elements be expected to successfully establish public security without significant U.S. military
participation.

- **Create a structure for rapid assistance.** The USG should examine Britain's Department for International Development's
(DFID's) cooperation with the British armed forces to see how
USAID's disaster assistance response teams (DARTs) might interact more directly with U.S. military assistance operations.

Improving Interaction with IOs and NGOs

- **Coordinate at the strategic level.** CENTCOM liaisons during
the initial stages of OEF facilitated unprecedented communication between the military and IOs and NGOs. We recommend
that this process be further institutionalized.
- **Coordinate at the field level.** NGOs, UN agencies, and independent IOs are reluctant to coordinate with U.S. forces engaged in combat operations. USAID/DART should act as the
formal coordinating point with the NGO/IO world.
- **Simplify the information flow.** Afghanistan reinforced the need
for an information management strategy and infrastructure. A
formal system recognized by all the players (government and
nongovernment alike), with full interoperability across different
databases, should be established. This will require a major effort
to overcome the problem of classification restrictions.

Turning Lessons Learned into Lessons Applied

We recommend that decisionmakers take the following actions to
apply lessons learned:

- **Incorporate lessons into doctrine and training requirements for
DoD and USAID.** The Office of Foreign Disaster Assistance
(OFDA) and USAID Policy and Program Coordination
(AID/PPC) could incorporate the lessons for USAID. The
National Defense University (NDU), the National Foreign

Affairs Training Center (NFATC), and USIP could play a similar role for the USG interagency process as a whole.

- **Encourage the development of a common NGO and IO doctrine.** IOs and NGOs should focus on developing a baseline doctrine for CMOs. The existence of such a framework, even if it were not universally endorsed, would enable greater cooperation with the U.S. and other professional militaries. Canada's Pearson Peacekeeping Center and USIP could perhaps facilitate this effort, providing a neutral venue for engagement.

- **Develop joint doctrine for humanitarian-type assistance.** In the same way that joint doctrine was necessary for the U.S. military, an integrated doctrine for complex contingency operations (CCOs) on the USG's civilian side, including CCOs undertaken in connection with combat operations, is required.

- **Integrate civilian-military planning.** The USG should develop a standing National Security Council (NSC)–centered mechanism for interagency coordination of complex operations, including those undertaken as part of combat operations, that would apply to future situations in the war on terror.

- **Create a "reserve" civilian reconstruction force.** A civilian reconstruction force with cadre personnel on retainer for rapid deployment would help establish USG civilian efforts in CCOs.

- **Integrate CMO/humanitarian-type assistance strategies into military doctrine.** If the Afghanistan experience is likely to be a model for future efforts, the structures used in Afghanistan (the Coalition Joint Civil-Military Operations Task Force [CJCMOTF], coalition humanitarian liaison cells [CHLCs], and provisional reconstruction teams [PRTs]) should be examined in light of new doctrine that takes lessons from this experience.

- **Develop guidelines for conduct of CCOs.** Military/USAID/NGO/IO cooperation in developing CCO guidelines informed by the experience in Afghanistan—and in exercising them—would encourage a more cooperative environment.

Acknowledgments

The research team (RAND and USIP) collaborated closely with a third group of analysts from the U.S. Army War College Peacekeeping and Stability Operations Institute (PKSOI). We are grateful to PKSOI for sharing its interview notes from a concurrent project on related themes and for facilitating the travel of team members to Afghanistan. Since its establishment in 1993 by the Chief of Staff of the U.S. Army, PKSOI has pursued a mandate to explore the military aspects of peacekeeping missions around the world. Its engagement, though not formally a part of this project, was invaluable. In particular, the research team would like to thank Col. William Flavin (U.S. Army, Ret.) of PKSOI for his significant assistance throughout the project.

The research team also wishes to thank all of the participants in its October 7–8, 2002, workshop on civil-military relations in Afghanistan for their insights. We also thank those we interviewed in Afghanistan in the course of the study, including the leadership of both civil and military organizations, as well as representatives of international organizations and the USG. In the United States, interviewees included personnel at USG agencies such as the Department of State, DoD (including U.S. Central Command and other U.S. military organizations and structures), and USAID, and at various offices of the United Nations, including the World Food Program (WFP), the Office for the Coordination of Humanitarian Affairs (OCHA), the Department for Political Affairs (DPA), and the Department for Peacekeeping Operations (DPKO). We would also like to thank the U.S. Mission to the United Nations for facilitating visits to UN Headquarters in New York. Representatives of the NGO community also informed this study at various stages during its conception and research.

The sponsors of this research effort, the Office of Stability Operations in the Office of the Secretary of Defense, led by Dr. Joseph Collins, and Tish Butler, in USAID's Policy Planning Office, are thanked for asking the question in the first place and for their support as we carried out our research. We are particularly grateful to Michael McNerney from the Office of the Secretary of Defense (OSD) and Ross Wherry from USAID for their support and assistance.

Miriam Schafer and Sarah Harting at RAND facilitated research, ensured that meetings and conferences went smoothly, proofread documents, and generally kept the process moving. Without them, this research would never have been completed. Iris Pilika and, later, Erica Johnston and Elise Murphy assured that the process moved forward for USIP.

In thanking all of these people and the many others who contributed to this report, the authors note that any errors or omissions in the finished product are their own.

Glossary

ACBAR. Agency Coordination Body for Afghan Relief. Coordinated NGO aid efforts launched from Peshawar, Pakistan.

AIMS. Afghanistan Information Management System. Was created to provide a comprehensive database of NGOs and IOs operating in Afghanistan.

ARCENT. U.S. Army Forces Central Command. The Army component headquarters for U.S. Central Command (USCENTCOM, or CENTCOM).

CCC. Coalition Coordination Center. Established at CENTCOM HQ in Tampa, Florida, during Operation Enduring Freedom (OEF) to coordinate activities with coalition partners. Also included liaison representatives from the U.S. Department of State, USAID, UNHCR, OCHA, WFP, and InterAction, an NGO umbrella group.

CCO. Complex contingency operation.

CENTCOM. U.S. Central Command (also USCENTCOM). One of nine unified combatant commands assigned operational control of U.S. combat forces. CENTCOM's area of responsibility includes 25 nations in the Horn of Africa, South and Central Asia, and the Northern Red Sea regions, as well as the Arabian Peninsula and Iraq.

CFLCC. Combined Force Land Component Command.

CHLC. Coalition humanitarian liaison cell. Staffed by Army civil-affairs specialists, the CLHCs' mission is to support humanitarian-type assistance efforts throughout Afghanistan. The first CHLC was set up in Islamabad to help coordinate the delivery of aid into Afghanistan by supporting information-sharing among various countries, groups, and agencies. Later, CHLCs were based in major cities throughout Afghanistan. They provided civil-affairs support to the coalition, sought to coordinate assistance efforts, and carried out coalition assistance and reconstruction projects.

CIMIC. Civil-military cooperation.

CIS. Commonwealth of Independent States. Made up of all the former Soviet republics except the three Baltic states. The CIS was founded in 1992.

Civil affairs. Military forces with the responsibility for liaison with civil authorities in a given area of operation. Civil-affairs personnel include specialists in every area of government, and they often have responsibility for reconstruction and humanitarian-type assistance activities.

CJCMOTF. Coalition Joint Civil-Military Operations Task Force. The coalition task force responsible for supporting humanitarian and humanitarian-type assistance efforts.

CJTF-180. Combined Joint Task Force 180. The U.S.-led coalition force in Afghanistan whose mission was to defeat and destroy al Qaeda and Taliban remnants. A combat-oriented mission.

CMO. Civil-military operation.

CMOC. Civil-military operations center. A mechanism through which military forces can support humanitarian activities and liaise with civilian assistance providers. In Afghanistan, CHLCs took the place of CMOCs.

DART. USAID disaster assistance response team.

DFID. Britain's Department for International Development.

DPA. United Nations Department for Political Affairs.

DPKO. United Nations Department for Peacekeeping Operations.

FEMA. Federal Emergency Management Agency.

HACC. Humanitarian Activities Coordination Council. Set up at CENTCOM in Tampa, Florida, during OEF as a daily forum for CENTCOM, UN agencies, and InterAction to address immediate-term crises.

HAWG. Humanitarian Activities Working Group. Established at CENTCOM as a nexus for CENTCOM personnel to interact with coalition military representatives, meeting two to three times per week.

HDR. Humanitarian daily ration. Food packets air-dropped by U.S. military forces into Afghanistan during OEF.

Humanitarian space. The ability of humanitarian aid–oriented organizations (both IOs and NGOs) to provide humanitarian assistance to populations in need. (This term poses difficulty and is often variously defined.) Impediments to humanitarian space include ongoing conflict and perceptions that aid organizations are aligned with belligerents.

Humanitarian-type assistance. Food, shelter, health care, and related assistance provided by military forces or other governmental entities, which may or may not be provided solely on the basis of need.

ICRC. International Committee of the Red Cross.

IDP. Internally displaced person.

IMTF. Integrated mission task force.

IO. International organization. Includes the entire UN family of organizations and also independent groups such as the IOM and the ICRC.

IOM. International Organization for Migration.

ISAF. International Security Assistance Force. The UN-mandated multinational force tasked with provision of stability assistance in Afghanistan, although its operations were limited to Kabul during the time covered by this report. ISAF was later expanded beyond the capital and placed under NATO command.

mujahidin (mujahedeen). (Literal translation: fighter for Islam.) Afghan armed resistance to Soviet occupation and the Soviet-backed Afghan government in the 1980s and early 1990s.

NGO. Nongovernmental organization.

Northern Alliance. Colloquial term for the United Front, a collection of anti-Taliban forces concentrated in the north and east of Afghanistan prior to OEF.

OCHA. United Nations Office for the Coordination of Humanitarian Affairs.

OEF. Operation Enduring Freedom. The U.S.-led military operation to defeat al Qaeda and the Taliban in Afghanistan, launched on October 7, 2001.

OHDACA. Overseas Humanitarian, Disaster, and Civic Aid. A DoD appropriation for providing assistance funding.

OSCE. Organization for Security and Co-operation in Europe.

OSGAP. United Nations Office of the Secretary General in Afghanistan and Pakistan. Set up after the 1988 Geneva Accords to foster an interim government in Afghanistan following the Soviet withdrawal in February 1989.

Pashtuns (Pashtoons, Pathans). The plurality ethnic group in Afghanistan, especially prevalent in the south and the east. Traditionally the politically dominant group. Also the majority in neighboring Pakistan's Northwest Frontier province and Baluchistan.

PRT. Provisional reconstruction team. Large mixed civilian (USG and Afghan government) and military teams whose aim is to help catalyze reconstruction beyond Kabul, enhance security, and expand the footprint of the Afghan government.

Tajik. A major ethnic group in northern Afghanistan, predominant in the northeast. The main ethnic group in the Northern Alliance (United Front) and heavily represented in the "power ministries" of the Karzai government.

Taliban. From *talib*, or (religious) student. The Islamic fundamentalist militia that swept to power in Afghanistan in the chaotic mid-1990s with Pakistani and Saudi backing.

SOF. Special Operations forces.

SRSG. Special Representative of the Secretary General (of the United Nations). In Afghanistan, Dr. Lakhdar Brahimi, head of UNAMA, served as SRSG from October 2001 through December 2003.

SWABAC. Southwestern Afghanistan and Baluchistan Agency Coordination.

UAE. United Arab Emirates.

Ulema (Ulama). Islamic clergy.

UNAMA. United Nations Assistance Mission in Afghanistan. Headed by the SRSG.

UNDP. United Nations Development Program.

UNHCR. United Nations High Commission for Refugees.

UNICEF. United Nations Children's Fund.

UNITAF. Unified Task Force.

United Front. A collection of anti-Taliban forces concentrated in the north and east of Afghanistan prior to OEF. See Northern Alliance.

UNJLC. United Nations Joint Logistics Center.

UNOCA. United Nations Office for the Coordination of Humanitarian and Economic Assistance Programs. UNOCA ostensibly (but unsuccessfully) coordinated UN agency assistance to Afghanistan in the early to mid 1990s.

UNOCHA. United Nations Office for the Coordination of Humanitarian Affairs. Also OCHA.

UNSCR. United Nations Security Council resolution.

UNSMA. United Nations Special Mission in Afghanistan. Established after the Strategic Framework.

USAID. U.S. Agency for International Development.

USCENTCOM. See CENTCOM.

Uzbek. A major ethnic group in north-central Afghanistan, the area abutting Uzbekistan.

WFP. United Nations World Food Program.

CHAPTER ONE

Introduction

The broad international humanitarian assistance effort in Afghanistan during the initial stages of Operation Enduring Freedom (OEF), from October 2001 to June 2002, was generally successful. A major—and anticipated—catastrophe was averted by the hard work of many actors, governmental and nongovernmental, civilian and military. Refugee flows were handled effectively, food was delivered to the hungry, and the first steps were taken toward stabilizing a country that had endured decades of war. But the overall success does not mean that the process could not have been improved or that there were not difficulties along the way. The perennial questions of what groups and what individuals should play which roles in providing humanitarian and humanitarian-type assistance, particularly the appropriate roles for military personnel, came into stark relief in Afghanistan. Coordination and cooperation between various assistance providers, while sometimes immensely successful, at other times was marked by tension over respective roles and lack of mutual understanding of each actor's perceived role.

In some ways, assistance provision in Afghanistan was unlike that in past operations. The most prominent differences resulted from the fact that military operations began on very short notice, providing little opportunity to plan for the role of assistance in achieving military and political goals. Other unprecedented elements included a lack of provision for humanitarian and humanitarian-type assistance in the mandates that authorized the coalition military force's deployment, the restriction of the International Security Assistance Force

(ISAF)—which did, in its mandate, incorporate such provisions—to the area immediately around Kabul, and security restrictions on movement of U.S. government (USG) civilians. While these circumstances may or may not be repeated in the future, they should not be seen as a shift in the paradigm for humanitarian and humanitarian-type assistance provision.

There were some parallels with past operations. The presence of multiple external military forces with different mandates and missions was not unprecedented. The absence of a local central government with the capacity to impose security and the rule of law was typical of past operations, as was confusion about the chain of command within the USG and between various in-theater agencies. The evident tension between assistance providers (and not only between civilians and military personnel) also was typical, stemming from the different cultures of organizations involved in assistance provision, their disparate mandates and paradigms for assistance provision, and their perceived competition for the scarce resources of funds, media attention, local professional staff, and so forth.

There were challenges that arose in Afghanistan that military and civilian planners and policymakers should regard as likely to occur in the future. The temporal coincidence of combat operations and assistance (including that provided by military forces) may become a new paradigm. The highly selective structure of U.S. military involvement and the bifurcation between a predominantly U.S. combat force and a predominantly international reconstruction, stabilization, and assistance effort may also be repeated. U.S. and military coalition forces were considered belligerents by international organizations (IOs) and nongovernmental organizations (NGOs), which hampered coordination. The ISAF, which operates under an international peacekeeping mandate, did not face this challenge. The proactive U.S. Department of Defense (DoD) involvement in assistance, including significant and early DoD budgetary commitments, is unlikely to end with Afghanistan. Future conflicts will likely require the military to maintain public order and security immediately after combat operations end, or perhaps while they are still ongoing.

Some things done for the first time in Afghanistan worked tremendously well and are likely to be repeated in the future. The unprecedented effort to involve civilian government agencies, IOs, and NGOs in aspects of planning, particularly inviting liaisons with U.S. Central Command (CENTCOM) headquarters, proved an effective way to better coordinate efforts and to increase mutual understanding. In fact, the success of this approach highlighted the inability to establish similar liaisons in the field, where they could have been equally helpful.

A consistent and far-reaching problem was the absence of clear, overarching policy guidance. This was a problem among U.S. agencies, within the U.S. military, and in the nongovernmental sphere. The *ad hoc* and improvised nature of the campaign resulted from the unique circumstances of this conflict. This situation led, however, to the absence of both adequate planning and clearly articulated guidance in a number of areas. The problem was exacerbated by the absence of a recognized process by which the U.S. administration could provide such guidance to its own government agencies—old mechanisms had lapsed, but new ones had not yet been put in place. Thus, planning followed implementation, and when a concrete plan was developed, awareness of it was insufficient.

Afghanistan has the potential to teach the USG (both its civilian and military personnel and organizations) and all those who interact with it a good deal about what is and what is not effective in a complex contingency operation (CCO). How inclusive should preintervention planning be, and how can effective liaison arrangements be created in difficult situations? How can military and civilian assistance providers find a *modus vivendi* in an environment of continuing combat operations? Tension about what humanitarian-type assistance the military should provide or even whether the military should provide, as opposed to facilitate, humanitarian-type assistance (and how it terms and defines its assistance efforts) reflects a real conflict between civilian (NGO and IO) and military planners. Overarching all of this is the question of public security: Whose responsibility is it, and under what circumstances? All of these factors had, and continue to have, a major effect in Afghanistan. The extent to which all the actors involved are willing and able to learn from the experience will help determine the success of future missions.

This report considers these questions, looking at the military, civilian USG, IO, and NGO actors' experiences in providing assistance in Afghanistan between September 2001 and June 2002. Based on the findings of this analysis, key issues are identified and recommendations for future operations are offered. It is hoped that this study will provide some guidelines that will enable a broad range of organizations to more effectively learn from Afghanistan.

CHAPTER TWO

Assistance in Times of Conflict: The Pre–September 11 Experience

Paradigms of Assistance: A Framework

Since the end of the Cold War, the U.S. military has participated in efforts to help disaster-stricken populations, end ongoing conflicts, and reform and rebuild post-conflict societies. This involvement has brought the military into frequent contact with the civilian missions operating in the areas in question. The civilian-military interaction has varied from cooperation and coordination in some cases to friction and contention in others. This chapter highlights the major historical points of friction between the civilian and military components of humanitarian assistance missions.

Lack of a common terminology has often led to misunderstandings, and even distrust, in humanitarian assistance efforts. IOs and NGOs often employ the term *humanitarian* to refer to a particular act being taken (i.e., humanitarian assistance, humanitarian emergency, humanitarian interventions). Within this community, however, there is no uniformity on the scope of the term. Some use it only for impartially provided relief, while others extend the usage into human rights activism and reconstruction. In general, these views suggest that the term *humanitarian* refers to the motivation of assistance provision, rather than the assistance itself. At the same time, the U.S. government and the U.S. military have traditionally used the term *humanitarian assistance* to refer to assistance that provides food, shelter, health care, and similar aid to a needy population, as differentiated from, for example, military assistance. In this report, the term *humanitarian-type assistance* is used to indicate food, shelter, health care, and related assistance provided by U.S. military forces or other governmental entities, assistance that may or may not be provided solely on the basis of need.

The term *humanitarian space* is also not uniform in its connotation or usage. The general concept of *humanitarian space* refers simply to the ability of IOs and NGOS that are focused on humanitarian assistance to do their work without undue interference by combatants or governments. It is an ideal that is often unrealized. But given the frequent use of the term by professional IO and NGO practitioners, it is also used in this report, where it refers to situations of grave perceived threats to the ability of civilian assistance providers to function safely and effectively.

The U.S. military and USG policymakers also employ a number of contentious terms. *Nation-building* is one term that has generated much controversy, particularly in recent years. *Complex contingency operation* describes the problem rather than the efforts to reach a solution, and it provides little in the way of specification, since few military operations are not both complex and contingent. *Stability operations* is another term that is prone to be misunderstood. The purpose of such operations is, after all, to reform affected communities rather than to perpetuate their conditions—as *stability* might be understood to imply. There is no agreed common lexicon within civilian and military organizations, much less between them.

Despite an extensive history of collaboration between representatives of the U.S. government, the U.S. military, and IOs and NGOs, expectations diverged prior to the beginning of OEF in Afghanistan in October 2001. Each community embraces different cases as reference points for determining its respective role in such operations, and these communities generally draw different lessons from their respective experiences. These lessons can best be summarized by first considering the situations that call for humanitarian assistance and then looking at how various groups see some of the specific historical cases that have informed their viewpoints and approaches.

Natural Disasters

Occasionally, natural disasters precipitate humanitarian calamities that overwhelm the ability of civilian humanitarian assistance providers to address the needs of affected populations. The military's logistical and organizational capabilities, particularly heavy lift, are often useful in such emergencies. In these situations, the military acts in a humanitarian support role. There is no fundamental clash between the missions of the humanitarian assistance providers and the military. There may be some tactical friction points, but effective coordination can eliminate most of them. Effective mechanisms to facilitate civil-military cooperation in such scenarios include joint planning, liaison, and coordination centers.

Peace Operations

A peace operation presents a more complex environment for civil-military relations. Peace operations usually receive their legitimacy through a recognized international body (e.g., the United Nations [UN] Security Council). In a peace-enforcement mission, the military has to be prepared to engage in combat. Civilian humanitarian assistance providers expect the military to provide a safe and secure environment in which they can operate, but tensions may arise over the level of security to be provided. NGOs and IOs may want security at specific locations that they deem essential for their operations (e.g., ensuring the safe return of internally displaced persons [IDPs] or refugees), while military commanders may be in a position to provide only area security. Friction may also arise when the military provides humanitarian aid to populations as part of a "hearts and minds" effort to build consent among the locals (and thereby reduce threat levels). A single civil-military hierarchy can help alleviate these conflicts, but establishing such a hierarchy is not always possible, especially if the peace operation involves a multinational force. Formal mechanisms for coordination among military and civilian actors, both at senior decisionmaking levels and in the field, have proven to be effective substitutes.

Combat Operations

Combat operations present major challenges for effective civil-military cooperation. Military forces have the objective of defeating an opponent. Therefore, interaction between civilian humanitarian assistance providers and the military in combat operations is particularly sensitive. As one respected member of the NGO community explained, "In order . . . to carry out [our] mission effectively, it is critical that we maintain the trust of those whom we serve. It is essential to be accepted by communities for what we are: a non-governmental and independent entity focused solely on the welfare and development of ordinary . . . citizens."[1] While many NGOs, as a matter of principle, will not work with belligerents—a category that, in their view, includes all or most military personnel active in a combat zone—they nonetheless request that the combatants in a war zone provide a safe and secure environment in which they can operate. To rely on one or more of these combatants to provide such security can compromise the perceived impartiality of NGOs and IOs and may, ironically, increase risk to their personnel. However, there is often no other option. Thus, combat operations increase the inherent tension between military and civilian assistance providers, and even coordination must be handled with great delicacy. Discretion in contacts can reduce tensions; however, until the combat phase ends (and possibly even after that), tensions will continue.

Past Experience and Military Expectations

Since the fall of the Soviet Union, the U.S. military has been involved in a series of efforts intended to end conflict and reform and rebuild post-conflict societies. These operations, in which the military has developed closer, and sometimes contentious, relationships with IOs and NGOs, are described briefly below. They have become the guideposts for the military community in setting up their own

---

[1] Interview with NGO personnel, April 2, 2003.

framework for interacting with the civilian community in humanitarian emergencies.

Somalia

The U.S. and UN interventions in Somalia are particularly instructive examples, because they illustrate the danger of half measures. The first Bush administration originally intervened to protect the delivery of humanitarian aid, which belligerent clans in that failed state were plundering and the light UN Mission in Somalia (UNOSOM) was unable to protect. Catalyzing a coalition of the willing in the Unified Task Force (UNITAF), U.S. forces not only provided protection, but also facilitated the delivery of aid by opening ports and airfields and repairing roads and bridges. Disarmament of belligerents had not progressed very far when the United States withdrew most of its forces and a new UN command, UNOSOM II, assumed responsibility.[2] The United Nations had much less combat power but a far more ambitious mission, centering on implementation of accords that would produce a new central government. The United States supported the UN command with one battalion of light infantry and, later, Special Operations forces (SOFs) sent to capture an especially obstreperous clan leader. This reduced force sustained losses, most spectacularly in the October 1993 firefight where two Blackhawk helicopters were shot down and 18 U.S. soldiers were killed,[3] and it was not able to master the situation. The lesson was that the doctrines of unity of command and overwhelming force apply to complex contingencies as well as to conventional campaigns.

Somalia demonstrated the utility of civil-military operations centers (CMOCs), structures outside the tightly secured foreign civil-

---

[2] For more on the transition from UNITAF to UNOSOM II, see Nora Bensahel, "Humanitarian Relief and Nation Building in Somalia," in Robert J. Art and Patrick Cronin, eds., *The United States and Coercive Diplomacy After the Cold War*, Washington, DC: United States Institute of Peace Press, 2003, pp. 21–56.

[3] For an in-depth account of this incident, see Mark Bowden, *Black Hawk Down: A Story of Modern War*, New York: Atlantic Monthly Press, 1999.

military compounds that allow U.S. military forces to support and coordinate with civilian humanitarian aid organizations.[4]

Haiti

Haitian President Jean-Bertrand Aristide was overthrown in a military coup in September 1991, a scant eight months after he took office.[5] Both the Bush administration and the incoming Clinton administration opted for denunciation of the coup, other diplomatic efforts to restore democratic rule, and sanctions, but neither undertook decisive action. By summer 1994, waves of Haitian refugees were landing on Florida's shores, increasing public and political pressure for the Clinton administration to resolve the crisis.[6]

The UN Security Council resolution allowing an intervention in Haiti, UNSCR 940, passed on July 31, 1993, was contingent upon the force being multinational. The resolution allowed the force to "use all necessary means to facilitate the departure from Haiti of the military dictatorship" and mandated it to "establish and maintain a secure and stable environment."[7] Operation Uphold Democracy (1994) in Haiti also began with a U.S.-led, UN-mandated coalition intervention that later transitioned to a UN-led effort, the UN Mission in Haiti (UNMIH). Unlike the intervention in Somalia, in military terms at least, the intervention in Haiti was a success. It was planned as a "forcible entry," but Haiti's military junta stepped aside at the eleventh hour in the face of imminent invasion (including paratroop drops), allowing what would later be termed a *permissive environment*.[8] The central problem for U.S. forces was a breakdown in

---

[4] On this, see particularly Chris Seiple, *The U.S. Military/NGO Relationship in Humanitarian Interventions*, Carlisle, PA: U.S. Army War College Peacekeeping Institute, 1996; and Bruce R. Pirnie, *Civilians and Soldiers: Achieving Better Coordination*, Santa Monica, CA: RAND Corporation, MR-1026-SRF, 1998.

[5] Roland I. Perusse, *Haitian Democracy Restored, 1991–1995*, New York: University Press of America, 1995, p. 13.

[6] Ibid., p. 85.

[7] Ibid., p. 97.

[8] Ibid., p. 105.

civil order following the disbanding of a corrupt military/police force. The troops from the 10th Mountain Division and other units had been prepared for combat, and the shift in mission parameters at the last minute made rules of engagement confusing to many soldiers, particularly when Haitian police attacked Aristide supporters and the U.S. troops were not allowed to intervene.[9]

However, these snags were dealt with quickly by Gen. Hugh Shelton, the force commander, who ordered that actions by police and auxiliaries must end.[10] Soon U.S. military police were conducting joint patrols with Haitian counterparts. In the countryside, U.S. Special Forces exercised quasi-governmental powers. American troops conducted operations, including a crackdown on pro-junta militias, to assure that the return of President Aristide could go forward smoothly.[11] U.S. forces also undertook emergency repairs to Haiti's dilapidated infrastructure, including restoring electrical power to Port-au-Prince. The U.S. Departments of State and Justice guided programs to create a new professional police force that would respect human rights.

Ultimately, the U.S. force strength reached 19,600 soldiers and marines. Before the United Nations assumed overall responsibility in 1995 (with continued U.S. force participation), the U.S. military command hosted a week-long training session for the new UN staff, helping smooth the transition. The remaining U.S. military, shrunk to a Special Operations task force, provided the core of the UN effort with military information support teams and civil-affairs teams, as well as a U.S. major general, who commanded the UN force.

Bosnia and Hercegovina
The NATO-operated and UN-endorsed military stabilization mission in Bosnia-Hercegovina, currently called the Stabilization Force (SFOR), has been operating in one form or another since 1995, al-

---

[9] Ibid., pp. 105–106.

[10] Ibid., p. 106.

[11] Ibid., pp. 110–111.

though it has steadily diminished in force strength over time. Initially, the United States agreed to be the lead element of NATO's Implementation Force (IFOR), contributing 20,000 of the 60,000 troops in the force. The United States announced at the outset of the operation that it would stay only a year in Bosnia, but this announcement was met with skepticism and was ultimately rescinded in late 1997. Under the Dayton Peace Accords, the United States and its allies created elaborate structures for the Bosnian effort, culminating in an immensely complex structure with roles for NATO, the Organization for Security and Co-operation in Europe (OSCE), the United Nations, a new Office of the High Representative (OHR) to coordinate international efforts, and a specially created Peace Implementation Council (PIC) to oversee the OHR and its work. It took almost two years for this structure to come into being and become fully functional. SFOR assures compliance with the military provisions of the Dayton Accords and guarantees internal security, preventing a resumption of conflict between the former combatants or intervention by neighbors. During the initial period, it also accomplished emergency repairs of the infrastructure, although responsibility for this task was quickly turned over to bilateral and multilateral donors. The World Bank and bilateral donors led by the U.S. Agency for International Development (USAID) developed a plan to revive the economy, using funds pledged at donors' conferences.

Despite much careful preparation, the effort was initially marred by a split between the civilian and military authorities, as well as a lack of clarity about NATO's commitment. SFOR took a strict constructionist view of its role, particularly on the arrest of indicted war criminals. As a result of this and other decisions made at the political level (including the decision to hold elections in 1996), progress beyond mere ceasefire was minimal in the immediate postwar period. This began to change with the arrival of the Blair government in Britain, which conducted the first forcible arrest of a war crimes indictee in the summer of 1997. A number of arrests have taken place since, although the senior indicted figures, Bosnian Serb Gen. Ratko Mladic and Bosnian Serb political leader Radovan Karadzic, have yet to be apprehended for trial by the International Criminal Tribunal for the Former Yugoslavia at The Hague.

The powers of the civilian high representative were augmented two years into the mission (December 1997), and each subsequent high representative has become more assertive in exercising his prerogative to be the final arbiter on interpretations of the Dayton Accords. Coordination between OHR and SFOR has improved considerably since the opening of the mission. At the senior level, civil-military cooperation between the high representative and the SFOR commander now works relatively well. Preservation of the peace in Bosnia has been remarkably successful, due largely to the overwhelming NATO force that was applied to the task. Progress in the construction of a functioning economy and government has been slow, in part because of divided responsibilities among international agencies in the civilian sector, but in larger part because of structural constraints (both perceived and real) within the Dayton Accords themselves. On the whole, progress has been considerable, but more in the latter years of the mission and less at the outset. At present, discussions are under way about handing the main international security responsibility to a European Union (EU) force, though it is likely that some American and NATO institutional presence will remain. The post-9/11 environment has forced a reassessment of earlier Bush administration plans to radically cut back the American regional presence.

Resulting Military Doctrine

The structure of U.S. military involvement in humanitarian and humanitarian-type assistance efforts has varied. Doctrine guides the activities of the military to some extent. U.S. military civil-affairs units, which have the responsibility for interaction with civilian agencies and support of humanitarian assistance delivery, structure their activities differently, depending on the given situation. In a peacetime intervention, for instance, with a government in place that U.S. forces are responsible for supporting, a situation of reasonable security is expected. Under such circumstances, civil-affairs forces are doctrinally guided to support civilian humanitarian assistance efforts. In times of war or active conflict, however, military doctrine assumes that the lack of security will preclude the involvement of civilian agencies and personnel. Therefore, there is less need to collaborate and coordinate with those agencies and a correspondingly more active assistance role for the military.

U.S. Army doctrine refers to military assistance provision as "humanitarian."[12] Specifically, this assistance involves short-term programs with three goals: (1) "to serve the basic economic and social needs of the people, and simultaneously promote support of the civilian leadership," while ending or alleviating human suffering; (2) to mitigate civilian unrest by improving the social and economic situation through such assistance activities as providing health care and building schools and roads; (3) to "supplement or complement" the local government's own efforts in providing relief.[13] This doctrine clearly states that military efforts "must not duplicate other forms of assistance provided by the U.S. government," potentially suggesting that military assistance efforts play a secondary role when others are under way. The doctrine is silent on duplication of or by NGO and IO programs.[14]

It is worth noting that military doctrine is also silent on the possible force-protection benefits of providing this sort of assistance, something that is more explicitly stated by some foreign civil-affairs personnel and by deployed U.S. forces.[15] Nor is the argument that these activities create a longer-term favorable impression of the

---

[12] The U.S. Army is not the only organization that has developed a doctrine for civil affairs. NATO, for example, is currently drafting Allied Joint Publication-09, NATO Operational Civil-Military Co-operation (CIMIC) Doctrine, though the final version has not yet been approved. However, this report focuses primarily on U.S Army doctrine, because Army personnel were the most directly involved in civil-affairs work in Afghanistan during the period examined.

[13] Department of the Army, *FM 41-10: Civil Affairs Operations*, Washington, DC: Headquarters, Department of the Army, 2000, paragraph 2-74.

[14] Ibid., paragraph 2-56.

[15] Interviews with ISAF personnel in the United Kingdom and Kabul, November 2002.

United States and U.S. forces, which will support better relations with the indigenous population in the future, made explicit. Yet both factors have been cited by U.S. military personnel as among the reasons for undertaking such activities.[16]

Past Experience and the Expectations of Civilian Actors

Prior to OEF in Afghanistan, civilian humanitarian assistance providers had accumulated extensive experience in collaborating with U.S. forces in responding to man-made disasters. Indeed, the term *humanitarian intervention* connoted a symbiosis between the military and humanitarian instruments of U.S. foreign policy. Large international humanitarian and reconstruction operations in Kosovo and East Timor helped establish patterns of interaction that were built on an assumption of cooperation in a context where U.S. forces were a part of a UN-sanctioned international peacekeeping operation, rather than a party to the conflict.

Kosovo

Kosovo is one of the main reference points in the IO/NGO community's worldview, reflecting its preferred mode of interaction with the military in humanitarian emergencies. The events of 1998–1999 in Kosovo contained elements of both combat and peace operations. During the bombing, NATO was a combatant, and afterwards, following a Serbian/Yugoslav withdrawal in June 1999, NATO forces entered and occupied Kosovo on a peace-enforcement mission under UNSCR 1244.

NATO's Kosovo Force (KFOR) was mandated to maintain security following the evacuation of Yugoslav armed forces,[17] and its force structure was designed to deter a hostile Yugoslav Army (VJ).

---

[16] Interviews with U.S. military personnel, spring, summer, and fall 2002.

[17] UNSCR 1244 can be viewed at www.usip.org/library/pa/kosovo/adddoc/kosovo_unsc 1244.html.

KFOR's presence improved public security, and for the first months of the mission, it was the only source of order.

The civilian peace mission, the UN Mission in Kosovo (UNMIK), was mobilized on short notice but took time to assemble. This left it at a great disadvantage vis-à-vis the military's capacity to act in the initial stages of the operation. KFOR filled the vacuum. The civilian police component of the mission required many months to become operational. The UN High Commission for Refugees (UNHCR) administered one of UNMIK's four "pillars," overseeing humanitarian efforts, including refugee return. This role was to be coordinated with the other essential aspects of the overall mission: civil administration (administered by the United Nations), institution-building (administered by OSCE), and reconstruction (administered by the EU).[18] UNHCR and other humanitarian aid agencies had planned for a phased return of refugees, but instead the process was spontaneous, taking place in a matter of weeks after Yugoslav forces had left. There were two principal points of friction between the civilian and military actors involved in the Kosovo operation: security and the military role in assistance.

Security Gap. The focal point of civilian humanitarian aid organizations' discomfort with KFOR was the lack of security, in particular for the Serb and Roma minority groups.[19] Since the civilian police component of the mission was slow to become operational, KFOR filled the security vacuum.[20] Civilian humanitarian assistance organizations considered the role of the military as the guarantor of security to be paramount and were concerned that KFOR was occupying itself with *ad hoc* humanitarian efforts at the expense of pro-

---

[18] Larry Minear, Marc Sommers, and Ted van Baarda, *NATO and Humanitarian Action in the Kosovo Crisis*, Providence, RI: Thomas J. Watson Institute for International Affairs, Brown University, Occasional Paper No. 36, 2000, p. 7.

[19] Ibid., p. 28.

[20] The international civilian police component of UNMIK is still viewed by many observers as largely ineffectual in its role.

viding an overarching security umbrella under which civilian humanitarian aid organizations could operate.[21]

Direct Assistance by Military Forces. NATO forces in Macedonia and Albania acted in a humanitarian support role for UNHCR and the NGO community, transporting food through unsafe areas, guarding aid warehouses, and protecting civilians. Until the end of the conflict, there was no UN sanction for these NATO activities.[22] NATO both assisted and, to an extent, competed with traditional humanitarian assistance providers such as UNHCR and the NGOs.[23] This challenged the impartiality of many IOs and NGOs, since cooperation with NATO in providing humanitarian assistance could be construed as aiding a belligerent in an escalating war.[24] There were hundreds of thousands of ethnic Serbs from Croatia and Bosnia living in Serbia and Montenegro, and some civilian humanitarian aid organizations felt constrained in their activities to assist this group while at the same time working with NATO in providing humanitarian assistance to Kosovars.[25] Also, some humanitarian workers suspected that KFOR's motivation was merely to "show the flag," driven by domestic political imperatives to justify for citizens back home why KFOR was there.[26] Other humanitarian assistance workers worried about the blurring lines between military and humanitarian roles. Moreover, NGOs viewed military efforts in the humanitarian sphere as inordinately expensive and believed that the resources would be better spent on their own more-experienced personnel and cheaper programs. Finally, armed forces tended to treat UNHCR as a single

---

[21] Different KFOR sectors (and contingents) carried their own reputations for provision of public security, relations with civilian humanitarian aid organizations, and general professionalism. According to feedback from internationals and locals in Kosovo, the British forces seemed best able to balance the full spectrum of these roles. See Minear, Sommers, and van Baarda, p. 30.

[22] Ibid., pp. 22–24.

[23] Ibid., p. 17.

[24] Ibid., p. 15.

[25] Ibid.

[26] Ibid., p. 30.

reference point for all civilian humanitarian aid organizations, alleg-edly denying NGOs their own voices.[27] In late April 1999, NATO concluded a Memorandum of Understanding with UNHCR, recog-nizing UNHCR's primacy and enumerating tasks for NATO troops within a framework defined by UNHCR. Some humanitarian work-ers viewed UNHCR as having been co-opted. Others saw this as *post hoc* formalism, because the situation was already being addressed on the fly by humanitarian workers and troops on the ground.[28] Civilian humanitarian assistance providers and KFOR reached a *modus vivendi* within six weeks of the cessation of hostilities.[29] While efforts such as the agreement between UNHCR High Commissioner Sadako Ogata and NATO Secretary General Javier Solana helped define relations at a senior level, the most effective coordination and division of labor occurred in the field.[30] Daily coordination between the UNMIK Special Representative of the Secretary General (SRSG) and the commander of KFOR was essential for this purpose.

East Timor

East Timor fits squarely in the peace-enforcement category. The In-ternational Force in East Timor (INTERFET) was authorized—though not organized or commanded—by the United Nations to provide security after the August 30, 1999, independence plebiscite provoked violence by anti-independence militias trained and sup-ported by Indonesian forces.[31] In October, UNSCR 1272 created the UN Transitional Authority in East Timor (UNTAET), which took over the mission from INTERFET. UNTAET had a pillar structure that included a peacekeeping force and a humanitarian effort under the UN's Office for the Coordination of Humanitarian Affairs

---

[27] Ibid., p. 19.

[28] Ibid.

[29] Ibid., pp. 30–31.

[30] Ibid., p. 20–21.

[31] UNSCR 1264 authorized this force under Chapter VII of the UN Charter to employ "all necessary measures" to restore order in East Timor and confront the militias. (Ibid.)

(OCHA). Once INTERFET was phased out in favor of UNTAET's peacekeeping force, there was unity of command of both civilian and military assets under the SRSG.

Civil-military coordination efforts began early with INTERFET, preceding the deployment of the force.[32] The UN civil-military cooperation (CIMIC) team produced a pre-operation planning document explaining the objective: cooperation to coordinate efforts in support of humanitarian objectives and to garner military support for humanitarian efforts.[33] The initial meeting between the force commander and the humanitarian coordinator on the day of the INTERFET deployment succeeded in highlighting the simultaneous (as opposed to sequential) character of military and humanitarian tasks, yet it fell short of achieving the full cooperation that the IOs and NGOs desired. These meetings, however, continued "almost daily."[34] After UNTAET was fully operational, the mechanisms were in place to address security issues in coordination with humanitarian needs.[35]

The friction points between civilian and military actors during the East Timor intervention were similar to those in Kosovo. They included the use of unique military assets (i.e., providing security) and the NGO/IO humanitarian assistance community's perception of military encroachment into humanitarian missions. The security gap was the premier issue, requiring improved communication and

---

[32] Michael Elmquist, *CIMIC in East Timor—An account of Civil-Military Cooperation, Coordination and Collaboration in the Early Phases of the East Timor Relief Operation*, Geneva: United Nations Office for the Coordination of Humanitarian Affairs, 1999, available online at http://www.reliefweb.int/ocha_ol/programs/response/mcdunet/0esttimo.html.

[33] Ibid.

[34] Ibid.

[35] On the day of the INTERFET deployment, the force commander and the humanitarian coordinator met. The INTERFET commander viewed his responsibilities, defined as "to restore peace and security in East Timor, to protect and support UNAMET in carrying out its tasks, and within force capabilities, to facilitate humanitarian assistance operations," sequentially. The humanitarian coordinator disagreed. He argued that such assistance was not a secondary or sequential goal to providing security and that "the military task could not be successfully accomplished unless it was complemented by immediate humanitarian relief." (Ibid.)

coordination. Given the continued existence of hostile militias interfering with the aid effort, security for the humanitarian aid community was essential. INTERFET initially resisted providing escorts for humanitarian convoys and later asked for 48 hours' notice, which the IOs and NGOs found impractical.

Summary of IO/NGO Paradigms

The "international community" intervened forcibly in both Kosovo and East Timor to address humanitarian catastrophes that were political in origin. In both cases, civilian humanitarian assistance providers from IOs and NGOs relied on international military forces for both security and logistical support, particularly in the period immediately following the interventions.[36]

In both Kosovo and East Timor, multinational military forces were initially the sole source of security. They had capacities without which civilian aid providers could not operate. In Kosovo, many IO and NGO workers believed that KFOR was slow to address the public security need. Civilian humanitarian aid organizations want the military, under an internationally recognized mandate, to provide a "secure environment" for refugees, returnees, and humanitarian aid workers. They would also like the use of military logistics, equipment, and manpower when these are needed to overcome critical bottlenecks in providing assistance.

Nonetheless, these international interventions provided a basis for collaboration between civilian and military forces. Some civilian humanitarian aid providers had the sense that they and the military were "all on the same team; that they often had complementary objectives."[37] Both the Kosovo and East Timor experiences also led NGOs and IOs to believe that a template for cooperation in future interventions had been established. Basic expectations of the civilian

---

[36] Minear, Sommers, and van Baarda, p. 18; Elmquist.

[37] Interview with NGO personnel, April 2, 2003.

humanitarian aid community based on the Kosovo and East Timor experiences included the following:

1. Military intervention would be backed with a UNSCR to legitimize a peacekeeping operation (even if there had been a combat element in the mission before this stage).
2. There would be some prior civil-military planning to define roles in the provision of humanitarian assistance, along with some end-state planning.
3. The military's role would increasingly revolve around providing a safe environment for NGOs and IOs, enabling them to deliver humanitarian and other forms of assistance.
4. NGOs and IOs would be able to preserve their neutrality and integrity in their operations (i.e., maintain their humanitarian space).
5. Coordination on the ground would be structured through a UN-led mechanism that would help coordinate the efforts of IOs and bilateral government donors, yet would allow NGOs to operate freely or coordinate as they saw fit.

Implications for Operation Enduring Freedom

The military and civilian positions, perceptions, and reference points with regard to both their respective roles and their interaction with each other clearly differ on issues ranging from mandate and doctrine to lessons learned and even cases cited. Yet there is also a desire on both sides to cooperate and coordinate. Both the differences in perceptions and the desire to overcome them are further highlighted by the case of Afghanistan.

The civilian IO and NGO community, having the Kosovo and East Timor missions fresh in its mind, came to the coalition intervention in Afghanistan with the expectation that there would be a clean transition to a post-conflict phase, in which cooperation with coalition forces could go forward as it had in previous peace-enforcement operations. Instead, it was presented with a continuing combat scenario.

The U.S. military, too, expected cooperation with civilian aid providers. Nevertheless, its doctrine called for "humanitarian" action in support of military and political goals, which differs fundamentally from the civilian preference for impartial, unprejudiced alleviation of acute suffering. This, along with the fact that the military continued to act in a combatant role without a UN mandate, limited the room for cooperation with IOs and NGOs.

Overall, the level and quality of interaction between the military and the civilian community vary, depending on the nature of the operations and, more specifically, on the nature of the involvement of the military in these operations. In natural disasters, military and civilian missions are essentially the same: to provide immediate relief to the affected populations. Specific tasks may differ given the different resources and capabilities each community possesses. In peace operations, where military forces have a mandate to provide a safe and secure environment, military and civilian missions are largely congruent and, to a large extent, sequential. When U.S. military forces engage in combat operations, however, inevitable conflicts arise. Because the nature and extent of the friction points vary considerably, methods used to address them must be adapted accordingly. Over time, as circumstances evolve that necessitate a change in the nature of the military mission, the civil-military interaction needs to evolve accordingly.

CHAPTER THREE

Afghanistan Before Operation Enduring Freedom

The Humanitarian Situation

The massive humanitarian problems of Afghanistan long preceded the post-9/11 American military campaign. Indeed, the U.S. attacks in Afghanistan represented the beginning of improvements in what was a very bleak humanitarian situation. As a UN official reported: "The basic facts of the Afghanistan humanitarian crisis by now are well known. Six to seven million people are estimated to be extremely vulnerable due to three years of severe drought and more than twenty years of war. The economy is shattered and offers very few employment opportunities."[1]

The UNDP/UNOCHA (United Nations Development Program/United Nations office for the Coordination of Humanitarian Affairs) Weekly Update of September 12, 2001, noted that there was internecine conflict in 17 of Afghanistan's 32 provinces.[2] At that time, about 75 international UN staff were providing humanitarian assistance from six locations in the country: Kabul, Jalalabad, Kanda-

---

[1] Prepared remarks of Mike Sackett, Regional Humanitarian Coordinator for the Afghan Crisis, at a conference co-sponsored by UNDP, the World Bank, and the Asian Development Body, November 27–29, 2001, available at http://www.pcpafg.org/reconstruction/document_paper/Mike_Sackett.pdf.

[2] *UNDP/UNOCHA Assistance for Afghanistan Weekly Update*, Issue No. 429, September 12, 2001, available at http://www.pcpafg.org/news/weeklyupdate/2001_Issues/update2001_09_12_429.shtml.

har, Herat, Mazar-e-Sharif, and Faizabad.[3] Several hundred international NGO personnel were also working throughout the country.[4]

The United Nations and the NGOs were attempting to address a deepening humanitarian crisis among the six million vulnerable people, including one million IDPs and countless more who were too weak or poor to leave their villages or homes. The weekly report noted: "If, as seems likely, the situation continues to deteriorate in the coming year, Afghanistan is set to become the worst humanitarian crisis in the world."[5] Earlier that year, the UN's special coordinator on internally displaced people, Dennis MacNamara, declared that Afghanistan had the highest rate of population displacement globally.[6]

Hundreds died from exposure in IDP camps, and even more died from malnourishment and illness. In 1999, over 3,000 mine-related injuries were reported. Primary school enrollment rates for boys were estimated at 39 percent; enrollment for girls was as low as 3 percent. It was estimated that there was one doctor per 50,000 people in Afghanistan (in fact, this was actually unrealistically optimistic because of the extremes in population distribution and density in the country). Twenty-five percent of all children died before their fifth birthday, and an estimated 15,000 women died each year during childbirth. NGO and IO efforts—relying heavily on American funding—provided what social infrastructure there was in the country, as the Taliban and other local governments never attempted to address these social needs. About four million Afghans were dependent on

---

[3] "UN Evacuates Afghanistan Staff," BBC News, September 12, 2001, available at http://news.bbc.co.uk/2/hi/south_asia/1539196.stm

[4] There was an overall cap on the number of UN aid workers in Afghanistan after the United Nations' withdrawal. (Interviews with UN personnel, April 23, 2003.)

[5] UNDP/UNOCHA Assistance for Afghanistan Weekly Update, Issue No. 429, p. 2.

[6] Kate Clark, "Afghans Are the World's Most Displaced People," BBC News, April 24, 2001, available at http://news.bbc.co.uk/2/hi/south_asia/1294482.stm.

food aid, of which the United States provided 40 percent, according to the UN's World Food Program (WFP).[7]

Washington increased U.S. assistance to Afghanistan through the spring and summer of 2001, in response to the growing humanitarian crisis. In May 2001, Secretary of State Colin Powell announced a new $43 million U.S. aid package, which included food aid, shelters, and health care, to be distributed by the United Nations and NGOs. Underscoring the gravity of the humanitarian situation, he said: "If the international community does not take immediate action, countless deaths and terrible tragedy are certain to follow." Despite its refusal to recognize the Taliban regime and its continuing pressure for the handover of Osama bin Laden, the United States was the largest single donor of humanitarian aid to Afghanistan.[8]

Afghanistan was a failed state economically, as well. The diversion of economic resources and means of production from general welfare to personal gain and/or supporting the internecine war efforts was staggering. The only work available for many was either direct involvement in or support of one of the armed factions inside Afghanistan, perhaps in combination with low-level participation in the opium trade. There was little governance of any sort, resulting in large-scale criminal activity and victimization of at-risk populations. There was no transportation or communications system in the country, and industries, education, and commerce sectors all suffered from either malign neglect or direct exploitation for political and military ends.

In a summary report on September 6, 2001, the Office of the UN Coordinator for Afghanistan asserted:

> Human suffering in Afghanistan has largely outstripped the capacity and resources of the aid community due to both the magnitude and the depth of the crisis. The catastrophe is a

---

[7] "U.S. Officials on Rare Afghanistan Visit," BBC News, April 18, 2001, available at http://news.bbc.co.uk/2/hi/south_asia/1283316.stm.

[8] "U.S. Announces Afghan Aid Package," BBC News, May 17, 2001, available at http://news.bbc.co.uk/2/hi/south_asia/1336958.stm.

gradually cumulative humanitarian disaster of enormous propor-
tions. Conflict, drought, displacement, grinding poverty and
human rights abuses add up to a deadly combination. Despite a
well thought out strategy in 2000, it has been impossible for the
aid community to respond to the extent necessary in all areas of
the country. The aid community has not had the resources, the
capacity, or the personnel to do so."[9]

A linkage to al Qaeda was obvious immediately following the
9/11 attacks on the United States, and military intervention—at the
very least, an operation to kill or apprehend al Qaeda founder Osama
bin Laden—seemed likely. The NGO and IO presence in Afghanistan was withdrawn soon after September 2001, though many local
employees remained. Thus, the primary distribution networks for
food assistance and other aid before the intervention were effectively
nonfunctional when U.S. forces entered Afghanistan. To fill this humanitarian vacuum, the U.S. military began building its own systems
for humanitarian aid even before it was on the ground. The civilian
post-intervention response faced considerable impediments to access
and coordination because of the ongoing combat and the further
degraded security situation. This made partnership or a coordinated
division of labor particularly difficult to achieve.

U.S. Humanitarian Assistance

As noted, well before September 11, 2001, the U.S. government was
engaged in dealing with this dire situation. USAID's engagement in
Afghanistan's food crisis dates back as far as 1979, the last year Afghanistan was able to feed itself. In September 2000, the United
States re-declared Afghanistan a complex humanitarian disaster, and
in February 2001, a disaster was declared for Afghan refugees in

---

[9] *UNDP/UNOCHA Assistance for Afghanistan Weekly Update*, Issue No. 428, September 6,
2001.

Pakistan. A USAID disaster assistance response team (DART) visited the region in March, and one DART was in place there by June, with another expected soon thereafter. During FY 2000 (October 1999 through October 2000), the United States provided $170 million in humanitarian assistance to Afghanistan, mostly in the form of food aid. USAID has the capacity to provide assistance both directly and through NGOs and IOs. Direct USAID assistance was primarily channeled through DARTs, the Office of Transition Initiatives (OTI), and two units of the Democracy, Conflict, and Humanitarian Assistance Bureau (DCHA). But most of the USAID assistance was provided indirectly, in the form of financial and material support to contractors and NGOs and commodities for distribution.

In April 2001, USAID's Office of Foreign Disaster Assistance (OFDA) sent a team into Afghanistan to assess the ongoing drought—the first visit by USG officials since 1988. USAID/OFDA responded by deploying a DART to Pakistan. There had been a DART on the ground almost continuously since March 2000,[10] assessing and coordinating emergency relief efforts, and an additional DART had been deployed to assist in Uzbekistan, Turkmenistan, and Tajikistan. USAID/OFDA and DCHA maintained a close relationship with the U.S. military and stationed a liaison officer with CENTCOM in October 2001. This established relationship allowed the DART to respond more effectively and more quickly than would have been possible otherwise.

Operating in and around Afghanistan during this period was difficult. Political instabilities and shifting alliances made the process of assessment and remedy difficult and dangerous. The DART's ability to travel in the region was greatly constrained by security concerns, limiting its ability to act as an interlocutor between the military and NGOs and IOs in the field. Despite this handicap, it played a key role in coordinating U.S. assistance and reporting on the worsening conditions within the country.

---

[10] Ibid.

International Political and Strategic Involvement

Neighboring States

Before September 11, 2001, the nature of international involvement in Afghanistan reflected the often tragic and always confused state of the internal struggle for political control that followed the withdrawal of Soviet forces in February 1989.[11]

The civil war that followed the departure of the last Soviet troops eventually led to the emergence of the Taliban (composed mostly of Pashtun refugees who had been living in Pakistan) in 1994. Between 1996 and 1998, the Taliban militarily overwhelmed the Northern Alliance of non-Pashtun minorities, disarmed a number of the other contending mujahidin militias, and took control of some 80 percent of the country, where it imposed a brand of Islamic fundamentalism on what it called the Islamic Emirate of Afghanistan.[12]

Only three countries officially recognized the Islamic Emirate of Afghanistan—Pakistan, Saudi Arabia, and the United Arab Emirates (UAE). The rest of the international community, including Muslim states, denounced either its aberrant form of Islam, its violations of human rights, or both. Pakistani and Saudi support was significant, however.[13] Pakistan, in particular, had long-standing strategic interests in Afghanistan. It has a sizable population of ethnic Pashtuns in the provinces bordering Afghanistan, including the Northwest Frontier province, which was only nominally under Islamabad's control. Most crucially for Pakistani political and military planners, a friendly, stable Afghanistan was seen as providing Pakistan with the strategic depth to allow its forces to respond to an Indian armored thrust across the Rajasthan Desert. The Taliban was seen as the group most likely to provide a more stable and compliant Afghanistan, and the fact that most of the Taliban's leaders had studied in Pakistani

---

[11] For greater detail on the history of international involvement in Afghanistan, see the Appendix to this report.

[12] John Esposito, *Unholy War: Terror in the Name of Islam,* New York: Oxford University Press, 2002, pp. 15–16.

[13] Ibid., p. 17.

madrasas (religious schools), primarily in Peshawar and along the Afghan border, was no small consideration.

Iran, bordering Afghanistan on the west, had been supporting Ahmed Shah Massoud and others. It saw the Taliban (rightly, as it turned out) as an anti-Shia force, and the Taliban's takeover in Kabul was a major blow to its objectives. Iran refused to recognize the new government in Kabul and continued its support of Massoud and Gen. Abdurashid Dostum, an ethnic Uzbek militia commander. It also continued to be concerned about the U.S. role in Afghanistan, which it saw as part of a broader U.S. strategy to surround and block Iranian influence in the region.[14] The massacres of local Shias and the murder of Iranian diplomats in Mazar-e-Sharif in 1998, along with later massacres of Shia Hazaras in Bamiyan province, only deepened Teheran's antipathy toward the Taliban.

Once the Soviet Union dissolved, Afghanistan also bordered three of its successor states—Turkmenistan, Uzbekistan, and Tajikistan. When the Taliban came to power, Tajikistan was already embroiled in its own civil war, with indigenous factions backed by some of Afghanistan's warring groups. Russia (and the other Central Asian states) feared that this conflict could spread throughout the region.[15] With the rise of the Taliban and the maturation of the neighboring countries' foreign policies, each pursued a different agenda. Turkmenistan developed ties with both the Taliban and the Northern Alliance. Leaders of an Islamist insurgency group seeking to overthrow the government of Uzbekistan found refuge in Afghanistan. And Russia, Uzbekistan, and Tajikistan all supported the Northern Alliance, in whose ranks the latter two's ethnic majorities predominated.

---

[14] Anwar-ul-Haq Ahady, "Saudi Arabia, Iran and the Conflict in Afghanistan," in William Maley, ed., *Fundamentalism Reborn: Afghanistan and the Taliban*, New York: New York University Press, 1998, pp. 118–134.

[15] Many in the new Central Asian states also feared that Russia's involvement in Tajikistan was partially driven by a desire to reassert control over what some in Russia's press called "the near abroad."

The United States and Russia

While the competition among regional powers for influence in Afghanistan shaped foreign involvement in pre-9/11 Afghanistan, competition for influence among powers from further afield also played a role. Throughout the 1980s, Afghanistan was a proxy location for superpower confrontation. In the end, however, the Soviet Union lost the military phase of the Afghan conflict and the United States lost interest. U.S. military assistance to the mujahidin ended in 1991, and economic assistance ended in 1993.

As the Taliban moved closer to power in 1996, U.S. diplomacy became more active. Washington was hoping to enhance its influence over the development and transportation of Caspian energy resources, and in addition, there was the hope that the Taliban might be able to suppress the Afghan drug trade and deliver a peaceful and stable Afghanistan after a decade and a half of strife.[16] This led the United States to take some small steps toward engaging the new Taliban authorities in Afghanistan. These actions appeared to place the United States with Saudi Arabia and Pakistan as supporters of the Talibs against the movement's enemies in India, Iran, and Russia. From the Taliban's perspective, there was hope that this American posture might eventually lead to U.S. diplomatic recognition.[17]

As fighting continued in Afghanistan and the commercial aspects of a gas pipeline project through Afghanistan to Pakistan became more doubtful, enthusiasm for recognition waned, both among corporate interests and inside the U.S. government. At the same time, more public attention was being drawn to the Taliban's treatment of Afghan women. It was soon clear that the United States was not seriously considering any moves toward recognition of the Taliban regime. This perception was confirmed when the United States bombed Osama bin Laden's camps in Afghanistan in 1998.[18]

---

[16] The Appendix to this report contains a more detailed discussion of the drug issue.

[17] Ahmed Rashid, *Taliban: Militant Islam, Oil and Fundamentalism in Central Asia*, New Haven, CT: Yale University Press, 2001, pp. 161–167.

[18] Ibid., pp. 170–175.

Following the dissolution of the Soviet Union in early 1992, Russia, for its part, behaved more like a regional power than a super-power. Rather than pursuing its engagement as part of an aggressive global agenda, Moscow approached Afghanistan from a defensive posture aimed at preventing the spread of radical Islam into Central Asia and Russia itself. When the Taliban rose to power, containing its influence inside Afghanistan became an explicit goal. In working (with Uzbekistan and Tajikistan) to funnel arms and supplies to the Northern Alliance, Russia aligned its interests with those of India and Iran. At the same time, however, the Russians were seeking to block U.S. inroads into Central Asia and Afghanistan, in particular Washington's support for non-Russian pipeline options for Caspian energy resources.[19] Obviously, an important subtext in all of this was Moscow's humiliating retreat from Afghanistan in 1989.

The United Nations

By the late 1990s, the UN presence in Afghanistan, in the form of the UN Special Mission in Afghanistan (UNSMA) and UNOCHA, was suffering from a competition between political and humanitarian imperatives. While the United Nations as a whole pursued peace in Afghanistan and applied sanctions against the Taliban regime, its humanitarian agencies and their NGO partners still had the task of assisting the population according to their mandates. The various UN agencies pursued different goals—the United Nations Security Council and UNSMA were the conduit for international criticism of the Taliban's brutal policies, while UNOCHA, UNHCR, and the UN Development Program (UNDP) sought to work around these barriers to reach Afghans in need. Seeking to better manage this tension, the United Nations adopted a Strategic Framework in early 1999 to "enhance the synergy between the United Nations political strategy in Afghanistan and the international assistance activities" and to "promote greater effective-ness and coherence in the international assis-

---

[19] Peter Marsden, *The Taliban: War, Religion and the New Order in Afghanistan,* New York: Zed Books, 1998, pp. 136–137.

tance program."[20] The premise driving the Strategic Framework was that "an effective peace-building strategy . . . can afford no 'disconnects' between the political, human rights, humanitarian and developmental aspects of the response. . . . Life-sustaining humanitarian assistance shall be provided in accordance with the principles of humanity, universality, impartiality and neutrality. . . . Assistance shall be provided as part of an overall effort to achieve peace." It further stated that reconstruction and development aid should be channeled "only where it can reasonably be determined that no direct political or military advantage will accrue to the warring parties in Afghanistan."

This attempt to square political with humanitarian imperatives did not address the concerns of some UN personnel and NGOs, who saw this policy as detracting from their own missions (and who preferred some distance from the United Nations' policy efforts). Penny Harrison, Head of Mission for Médecins sans Frontières–Holland in neighboring Tajikistan, said: "The Strategic Framework is predicated on the assumption that all the actors should speak with one voice, and adopt a coherent approach in which peace and assistance strategies are linked. But the assumption that a unified and principled approach is possible, required, or desirable among actors with very different mandates, charters and modes of operation raises some fundamental dilemmas." First and foremost, in her view, "the perception that humanitarian assistance can be used explicitly as a tool of peace-building or conflict management ignores the principle of impartial action—arguably the most fundamental principle we have." [21]

The humanitarian situation in Afghanistan continued its downward spiral after the adoption of the Strategic Framework, as the Taliban regime came under increasing international criticism and

[20] United Nations, "Strategic Framework for Afghanistan Endorsed by UN Agencies," January 4, 1999, available at http://www.reliefweb.int/w/rwb.nsf/s/3BA0FD484133864E852566 F000688B74.

[21] *The Strategic Framework and Principled Common Programming: A Challenge to Humanitarian Assistance*, Overseas Development Institute, September 4, 2001, available at http://www. reliefweb.int/w/rwb.nsf/s/55A1A592C36ABBF5C1256AD30056E380.

pressure because of its brutality, oppression of women, and cultural vandalism. Critics of the linkage of political and humanitarian priorities embodied in the Strategic Framework could cite the Secretary General's own admission that UN sanctions had a negative humanitarian effect on the ground. His July 2001 statement to the UNSC noted that the atmosphere of continuing warfare and drought were the primary factors adversely affecting humanitarian conditions. The report stated: "The period of sanctions has coincided with a series of adverse changes in the humanitarian operating environment (humanitarian space) in Afghanistan. Humanitarian agencies are concerned about their ability to continue to render assistance given the current trend of events. That this comes at a time of unprecedented humanitarian need is a source of vital concern." The Taliban impeded humanitarian access to women and other populations that were not Taliban priorities and more generally constrained the activity of humanitarian assistance IOs and NGOs. The report added: "These repeated assaults on humanitarian action became more frequent after the imposition of resolution 1333 (2000). They occurred in a period during which the Taliban frequently articulated complaints against the United Nations and the imposition of sanctions. This sequence of events shows that reactions to sanctions by the Taliban authorities contributed to the operating difficulties of humanitarian agencies." The Secretary General's report concluded that these difficulties were dwarfed by "other factors causing humanitarian suffering, most notably the unprecedented drought, the continuation of the conflict and the widespread deprivation of human rights."[22]

The effort to manage the competing mandates of the UN agencies in Afghanistan was bound to create conflict, and the tension between the political and humanitarian components of the mission became more pronounced as the humanitarian and political situations continued their downward trajectory between 1999 and 2001. UN

---

[22] United Nations Secretary General, *Report of the Secretary General on the Humanitarian Implications of the Measures Imposed by Security Council Resolutions 1267 (1999) and 1333 (2000) on Afghanistan,* July 13, 2001, available at http://www.reliefweb.int/w/Rwb.nsf/vID/7B5D0C534FE9DED85256A8B006F0324?OpenDocument.

sanctions, in creating a Taliban backlash against the UN system (and even NGOs), exacerbated the difficult position of humanitarian assistance providers.

Nongovernmental Organizations

The activities of NGOs in pre-9/11 Afghanistan influenced donor government attitudes toward Afghanistan because of the general lack of diplomatic presence in Kabul. In the early post-Soviet days, the International Committee of the Red Cross (ICRC) was the only humanitarian organization operating in Afghanistan. Many NGOs focused on assisting refugees in Pakistan and, to a certain extent, Iran. After the Geneva Accords, *ad hoc* groups began working cross-border programs, especially in mujahidin-held areas where refugees were expected to return. An interesting feature of this assistance was that much of it went through the hands of military commanders on the ground in Afghanistan, thus linking it, in the eyes of many Afghans, to the covert military support going to these same commanders.[23]

As USAID, UNHCR, and WFP began funding more-established NGOs to conduct their humanitarian assistance activities, NGO numbers grew. The overall effort suffered from the competitive nature of programs (and funding) often conducted under a veil of secrecy for security reasons. Competing political agendas of both recipients and donor agencies also contributed to the lack of transparency. Accountability was spotty because security concerns greatly hindered project monitoring. By the time the number of international and Afghan NGOs operating out of Pakistan reached 150, the agencies had formed a structured coordination framework with two regional bodies: the Agency Coordination Body for Afghan Relief (ACBAR), for programs originating from the Northwest Frontier province, and the Southwestern Afghanistan and Baluchistan Agency Coordination (SWABAC), for NGOs operating out of Baluchistan. ACBAR already was playing an important coordinating role that the

---

[23] Antonio Donini, *The Policies of Mercy: UN Coordination in Afghanistan, Mozambique, and Rwanda*, Providence, RI: The Watson Institute for International Studies, Brown University, Occasional Paper No. 22, 1996, p. 26.

United Nations Office for the Coordination of Humanitarian and Economic Assistance Programs (UNOCA) recognized when it arrived on the scene. Being a funding body, UNOCA could help improve the coordination process by giving institutional support to ACBAR and insisting on greater NGO professionalism and accountability.[24]

As the emphasis shifted to rehabilitation of physical infrastructure (e.g., clearing mines, restoring water, and rebuilding road and sanitation systems) and social infrastructure (e.g., restoring schools and health delivery systems), the NGOs ran into a cultural and values clash that would define their relationships with Afghans throughout the Taliban period. The radical Islamic ideology, which was virtually the only common feature among most mujahidin groups, gave pause to many NGOs. The rise of the Taliban only heightened this concern. In the area of education, including curriculum development, NGOs met stubborn resistance to the idea of equal access to education for all Afghans—in particular, girls. Similar difficulties arose in the health sector for NGO programs that targeted maternal and child health problems.

NGOs and donors faced a dilemma: They had to either suspend their programs as a matter of principle or compromise on issues relating to access of women to programs, services, and employment. In the end, only two agencies—the UN Children's Fund (UNICEF) and Save the Children—suspended their programs; the rest sought varying degrees of accommodation with the Taliban. Since the Taliban seemed indifferent to whether or not agencies continued to operate in Afghanistan, the NGOs and IOs had little leverage to force Taliban officials to change their opposition to agencies' employment of female staff and programs directed at female beneficiaries.[25]

Throughout their pre-9/11 involvement in Afghanistan, the NGOs could not shake the impression that their activities were involved with internal politics and the various war efforts. Indeed, Afghans did not regard the NGOs as neutral providers of humani-

---

[24] Ibid., pp. 45–50.

[25] Marsden, pp. 104–108.

tarian assistance but as partisan forces that took the side of non-Taliban mujahidin. Antonio Donini, who worked in the field for OCHA, pointed out another aspect of NGO involvement:

> Because of the politicized environment, the humanitarians usually operated in a political space instead of actively promoting humanitarian space and respect for humanitarian values. While this course of action may have been understandable but not excusable during the years of the Soviet invasion, the absence of a peace discourse remained a distinguishing feature of the Afghan scene well after the Soviet departure. NGOs and to some extent the UN did not make reconciliation and confidence-building a manifest objective of their humanitarian strategies.[26]

As the end of the Taliban era approached, the NGOs—despite the effective coordination framework that ACBAR represented—looked to their principal donors and boards of directors for ultimate political guidance. They were simply too geographically and culturally diverse to behave in a coherent fashion. The NGOs were critical of the United Nations' ability to coordinate among the many UN agencies operating in Afghanistan, let alone the NGO community, and they were suspicious of its political agenda.[27]

International Involvement in the Context of Political Conflict

International efforts to provide humanitarian assistance must be seen in the context of the competition for political influence in Afghanistan from the end of the Soviet occupation to September 11, 2001. It was never possible to disentangle the provision of such assistance from the political objectives of governments, IOs, or NGOs. For much of this period, these actors, either through choice or from necessity, had to rely on the political factions contending for power inside Afghanistan for the delivery of, or protection for, the assistance they were providing. Particularly following the Taliban's rise to

---

[26] Donini, p. 54.

[27] Michael Keating, "Dilemmas of Humanitarian Assistance in Afghanistan," in William Maley, ed., *Fundamentalism Reborn: Afghanistan and the Taliban*, New York: New York University Press, p. 143.

power, this affected the ability of NGOs to be perceived by the Afghans as neutral actors. The Taliban's human rights violations caused both donors and NGO boards to pressure NGOs not to work with Taliban forces and authorities. The result was that, whatever their intentions, NGOs were perceived by Afghans generally and by the Taliban in particular as partisan. This contributed to the increasing level of difficulty of delivering aid after the United Nations' temporary withdrawal in March 1998.[28]

Foreign governments were seen as even more partisan than the NGOs. Since few foreign governments had a diplomatic presence in Kabul during much of this period, and most supported particular (but not always the same) mujahidin groups for political purposes, the humanitarian assistance these governments provided was perceived by locals as tainted. The dependence of aid providers on local groups for security, along with their political motivations, convinced Afghans that something other than simply humanitarian goals was being served. The United Nations fared little better. Its inability to follow a consistent policy toward peacemaking and its unwillingness to integrate its political and assistance agendas were a recipe for failure of the UN peace process.

With the rise of the Taliban, many governments, IOs, and NGOs chose to operate in Pakistan among the Afghan refugee community. Those that continued to operate inside Afghanistan were either pro-Taliban (e.g., Saudi charities) or had to contend with such extensive Taliban restrictions that many programs simply could not be pursued. After the 9/11 attack on the United States, anticipation of retaliatory military action against Afghanistan caused a major evacuation of UN, other IO, and NGO expatriate staff from the country. Thus, the international community was caught with little effective on-the-ground presence when OEF began on October 7, 2001. However, its members had amassed considerable experience, both positive and negative, as a result of their previous engagement in the country.

---

[28] "UN Pulls Workers Out of South Afghanistan," BBC News Dispatches, March 24, 1998, available at http://news.bbc.co.uk/2/hi/dispatches/69086.stm.

CHAPTER FOUR

Civil-Military Operations: Planning and Cooperation Between September 11 and October 31, 2001

Military Civil-Military Operations Planning

During the initial planning and execution stages of OEF, CENTCOM's primary goals were the elimination of al Qaeda elements in Afghanistan and the concomitant destruction of the Taliban regime that harbored them. The limited nature of these objectives was strongly reinforced by the conventional wisdom throughout the U.S. policymaking community that the Afghan people would not tolerate a large coalition presence inside Afghanistan. Such a presence, it was believed, would trigger the Afghans' legendary wrath against occupiers and invaders.

These concerns, which were reflected in important strategic choices regarding the nature of the coalition military campaign in Afghanistan, stemmed from guidance from the most senior levels of the USG and DoD leadership. First, the primary foci of the campaign were to be the immediate phases of air strikes, support to anti-Taliban forces, and direct action missions against Taliban and al Qaeda targets. Any broader objectives, such as the development of an alternative political order in Afghanistan, would be left to later stages, as would their military aspects.[1]

Second, the military campaign was to be of limited duration. Just as the scope of the objectives was focused on al Qaeda and Mul-

---

[1] Interview with civil-military operations (CMO) planners, October 2002.

lah Omar's government, the coalition would seek to minimize the duration of its military involvement in Afghanistan.[2]

Third, the campaign was to be conducted with the minimum possible U.S. footprint on the ground in Afghanistan. Wherever possible, military missions would be conducted from neighboring countries or from elsewhere in the region. U.S. units that might operate inside Afghanistan would do so covertly or would limit their presence to small, discrete base camps isolated from Afghan society. Coalition commanders and planners constantly referred to the need to avoid "the mistakes of the Soviets," i.e., the need to limit the size and intrusiveness of the coalition military force in Afghanistan.

Thus, it is not surprising that there was little preparation for civil-military operations (CMOs) and activities in the initial phases of OEF. The tendency to downplay the role of such activities resulted from structural and bureaucratic factors. For example, there was no full-time CMO cell within CENTCOM. At the time OEF began, the few civil-affairs personnel assigned to the command were focused on humanitarian de-mining. A few weeks into the campaign, however, Reserve and National Guard CMO personnel were assembled to create and staff the CMO cell.

In time, the national command authority and the combatant commander recognized the importance of CMOs for the success of OEF. The strategic- and operational-level commanders wanted to make clear to the Afghan people that OEF was directed not against them, but against the Taliban regime and al Qaeda. It is unclear, however, that these commanders understood how to plan for CMOs and integrate them into the overall plan to achieve the desired CMO "effect." This could have been expected, given the limited expertise present at the various military command levels and the bureaucratic staff challenges inherent with Reserve civil-affairs elements. Still, the disconnect had significant implications for CMOs, most notably in the planning and deployment of the Coalition Joint CMO Task Force (CJCMOTF), discussed below.

---

[2] Interview with civil-affairs planners, May 2002.

Civil-Military Coordination

CENTCOM

Although planning did not include a large role for CMOs early in the campaign, there was a growing awareness that the U.S. military, coalition forces, and a variety of civilian governmental and nongovernmental actors in Washington, New York, and Tampa, Florida, would have to be involved, to varying degrees, in relief efforts in Afghanistan. Thus, coordination of these efforts would be imperative for their success. To facilitate coordination of military efforts among a large number of countries, CENTCOM had invited representatives of coalition states to come to its headquarters in Tampa to engage directly with CENTCOM personnel.

To support the assistance effort, the State Department and USAID were also present at CENTCOM headquarters, and they argued for the inclusion of representatives of IOs and NGOs as well. On their own initiative, within days of the start of combat, the NGO consortium InterAction (an umbrella organization of 160 NGOs), along with the United Nations' OCHA and WFP, sent staff members to the Office of the Secretary of Defense (OSD) and CENTCOM to discuss the need to "deconflict" their activities. The result was a proposal by the NGOs and the United Nations to post liaisons from various civilian humanitarian aid organizations at the Coalition Coordination Center (CCC) at CENTCOM headquarters. The CENTCOM commander approved the request, and USAID backed InterAction's participation financially.[3] This cell began functioning on October 10, 2004.

A variety of UN agencies, including WFP, OCHA, and UNHCR, sent representatives to the CCC. The UN Joint Logistics Center (UNJLC) also sent personnel to Tampa for two- to eight-week temporary duty, although UNJLC did not keep a representative there at all times. On occasion, the cell was also attended by representatives of USAID/OFDA and the State Department's Bureau of

---

[3] Interview with U.S. Army Peacekeeping and Stability Operations Institute staff, February 2004.

Population, Refugees and Migration (PRM).[4] Participation was debated within the United Nations because of concern that its impartiality might be compromised. In the end, liaisons from OCHA, WFP, and UNHCR, as well as InterAction, were assigned in mid-October. It was vital to the success of this enterprise, however, that their presence remain at a low level of visibility and that they focus on operational issues relevant to the United Nations and its mission.[5] By late October, the UN representatives had moved from their offices at CENTCOM headquarters into a trailer in the coalition village, which they shared with InterAction.[6]

Some UN and NGO representatives were frustrated with the liaison arrangement, because they believed that they were providing information to CENTCOM without receiving a free flow of information in return. The slow declassification of information vital to humanitarian operations also posed problems for these organizations. Especially in the initial stages, NGOs and IOs were frustrated by the inadequacy of information about population movements, the status of IDPs, and the disposition of forces. In some cases, information that had been provided by IOs such as WFP was classified once it was given to the military.[7] The high turnover rate of military personnel also required liaisons to go through the process of familiarization and education repeatedly.

Despite its limitations, the liaison arrangement had clear benefits, including a more expeditious exchange of information, regular access to senior commanders at CENTCOM, and the avoidance of "friendly-fire" incidents involving humanitarian facilities or personnel. Nevertheless, there were targeting mishaps. For example, while the ICRC did not post a liaison officer in Tampa, it provided information about its facilities, and still it was hit twice by U.S. airpower.[8]

---

[4] Ibid.

[5] Interviews with UN staff, April 23, 2003.

[6] Interviews with IO and NGO liaisons to CENTCOM, July 2002.

[7] Interviews with UN staff, April 23, 2003.

[8] We thank George Devendorf of Mercy Corps for this point.

The presence of liaisons also provided an opportunity for NGO and IO representatives to explain humanitarian principles and the way the NGO/IO humanitarian assistance community operated to the CENTCOM staff, whom international liaisons found to have a "thirst for knowledge."[9] These discussions influenced decisions about targeting, causing critical infrastructure items, such as certain airfields, to be excluded from the target list owing to their value for subsequent distribution of humanitarian assistance.

Civilian Organization Planning and Coordination in the Region
Soon after 9/11, international staff from all IOs and virtually all NGOs in the country were relocated from Afghanistan to Pakistan and other neighboring countries. After relocation, UN staff and NGOs planned for the expected refugee influx and postwar intervention, in anticipation of a clean break between the conflict and postconflict stages of the intervention. Operationally, the emphasis was on maintaining the capacity to communicate and coordinate with the local staff who remained in Afghanistan and continuing programs on a volunteer basis when security allowed. Continuing communication with local staff, and even the safety of these personnel, could have been jeopardized if the Taliban regarded international civilian humanitarian aid organizations and NGOs as an instrument of the coalition forces. Maintaining "humanitarian access" so that shipments of food could continue to flow across the border to vulnerable groups in Afghanistan required continuous interaction with Taliban representatives in Pakistan before and immediately following the start of OEF. Both IOs and NGOs felt that if coalition military representatives had attempted to conduct joint planning or coordination sessions in Pakistan, this would have breached impartiality unless the Taliban had also been invited to participate. In principle, the NGO/IO humanitarian assistance community could not align itself with any of the parties in the conflict.

---

[9] Ibid.

Despite this friction, some coordination had to occur. One example was the coordination and deconfliction of air traffic into Afghanistan. From the military perspective, CENTCOM was responsible for this, but a significant component of the mission was carried out in the early stages of OEF from Pakistan, where a variety of UN organizations and NGOs had set up temporary field headquarters after evacuating from Afghanistan. The structures set up in Islamabad were to be the model for the rest of the operation. U.S. civil-affairs personnel were deployed to Islamabad to support the humanitarian assistance efforts of various aid providers. The job of the civil-affairs personnel was to facilitate the sharing of information about security and routes into and out of Afghanistan, to coordinate the aid deliveries, and to deconflict them from other efforts. Initially comprising three soldiers from the British Army Civil Affairs Group and four from the U.S. 96th Civil Affairs Battalion, this structure was dubbed a coalition humanitarian liaison cell (CHLC).[10] In fact, there was little difference between a CHLC and a civil-military operations center (CMOC), the traditional term for such a structure. However, some of the NGO groups that were involved in aid flights were uncomfortable with the CMOC terminology and preferred something that downplayed the military aspect. This resulted in the coinage of CHLC.[11]

---

[10] "Afghanistan: Humanitarian Liaison Centre Opens in Islamabad," UNOCHA Integrated Regional Information Network, December 4, 2001, available at wwww.reliefweb.int/w/rwb. nsf/s/71A7E584ED3E85256B18007C6116; and interviews with U.S. military personnel, October and November 2002.

[11] Interviews with U.S. military personnel, November 2002.

CHAPTER FIVE

Assistance Efforts Between October 7 and December 5, 2001

Military Humanitarian-Type Activities

Humanitarian Daily Ration Drops

One of the most visible forms of early assistance by the U.S. military was the airdrop of humanitarian daily rations (HDRs) throughout Afghanistan. These drops began the same day the fighting did, October 7, 2001.

HDR drops have long been controversial. Opponents argue that they are an inefficient, ineffective, and expensive means of providing food aid. The international NGO/IO humanitarian assistance community objects to them on practical and philosophical grounds, claiming that HDR drops are ineffective in practice and inherently political in concept. Proponents assert that HDR drops are often the only way to get food to difficult-to-reach areas and that they are a highly effective means of demonstrating U.S. good will to the assistance recipients and other foreign audiences. In the case of Afghanistan, OSD and senior military personnel at CENTCOM claimed that the HDR drops were critical to an effective military campaign largely because of their demonstration effect. However, critics countered that such demonstrations were intended to maintain public support in the United States, not in Afghanistan.

More generally, however, NGOs, USAID, the State Department, and the CMO personnel at CENTCOM all opposed the HDR airdrops. They feared that there were insufficient data about the situation on the ground to enable effective food drops and argued that the cost of the HDRs was exorbitant in relation to their potential benefit.

The IOs and NGOs also were opposed on the basis of their conviction that the airdrops were essentially a psychological operation for political benefit—deliveries determined by opportunity rather than relative need. The very use of the term *humanitarian* in such an operation was impossible for most humanitarian assistance IOs and NGOs to accept. For an act to be regarded as legitimately humanitarian by these IOs and NGOs, the highest priority must be given to reaching the neediest groups first. The airdrops were perceived as being intended to benefit populations that were friendly to the coalition (particularly in Northern Alliance areas) and as more of a psychological operation to garner favorable publicity than an attempt to feed the starving.[1] Therefore, many in the United Nations and NGOs regarded HDR drops as purely military operations.[2]

The HDR drops also ran into a number of practical difficulties. There were initial concerns about the lack of knowledge regarding need and requirements on the ground, which raised questions about how target sites would be selected (they were selected on the basis of need, insofar as is known).[3] As one OCHA field worker noted, no knowledge was shared on where the HDRs would be dropped, or even on the criteria used to determine the drop zones.[4] Aircraft could not fly below 30,000 feet in the early stages of the conflict, due to concern about ground-fire risk. This resulted in high-altitude HDR drops, which raised questions about accuracy as well as the survivability of the packaging.[5] As a result, fewer drops were carried out than was originally intended.[6] To the extent that Taliban or other

---

[1] USIP-RAND Afghanistan workshop, October 2002; interviews with UN officials, April 23, 2003.

[2] Interviews with UN officials, April 23, 2003.

[3] Interviews with U.S. military personnel, November 2002.

[4] Interviews with UN officials, April 23, 2003.

[5] Indeed, some of the packaging did open upon impact, causing spoilage. The Taliban reported through its media that this was biological warfare by the United States. It is unclear what effect, if any, this disinformation by the Taliban had. (Interviews with UN officials, April 23, 2003).

[6] Interviews with U.S. military personnel, September and November 2002.

combatant forces were operating in a drop area, they—rather than the hungry public for whom the food was intended—inevitably became the unintended beneficiaries of this largess. This presented further public relations problems.

Even the color of the packaging was problematic. Many NGOs and IOs argued that the yellow packaging used in the early drops would be dangerously confusing, since cluster-bomb submunitions, also dropped in Afghanistan, were also yellow. Fears that civilians—particularly children—could be hurt or killed by a cluster bomb mistaken for an HDR package led to a decision to change the color of HDR packaging to salmon.[7] Military personnel dismissed the possibility that HDRs and cluster bombs could really be confused with one another.[8] However, some civilian assistance providers argued that the ability of Americans to tell the difference does not necessarily mean that people in a predominantly illiterate society with no foreknowledge of HDRs or of U.S.-manufactured cluster bombs could do the same. To quote one OCHA worker on the ground in Pakistan: "We thought it was important, the military didn't."[9] In any event, there were no recorded instances of Afghans mistaking cluster bombs for HDRs.

DoD pressed CENTCOM to increase the HDR drops, despite ongoing criticism from many IOs and NGOs. USAID continued to oppose the drops, expressing its position through interagency USG meetings. Other IOs and NGOs expressed their opposition to the drops through the IO/NGO liaison cell at CENTCOM headquarters in Tampa.[10] That cell then conveyed the messages up the chain of command to the Deputy CENTCOM Commander, to CENTCOM Commander General Franks, and, ultimately, to DoD.[11] Informing

---

[7] Interviews with UN officials, April 23, 2003; interviews with U.S. military personnel, November 2002.

[8] Interviews with U.S. military personnel, November 2002.

[9] Interviews with UN officials, April 23, 2003.

[10] Ibid.

[11] Interview with U.S. Army Peacekeeping Institute, April 23, 2003.

CENTCOM of actual World Food Program (WFP) food deliveries helped make the case for discontinuing HDR airdrops. In this case, collaboration among the IOs, NGOs, and civilian government representatives achieved results. HDR drops were soon scaled back, and those remaining were targeted predominantly in the north, in support of the Northern Alliance's advance.[12] However, this led some to question whether these HDR drops were truly humanitarian, since they were provided only to forces fighting in coordination with the United States.

Evaluating the success of HDRs is difficult. With a dearth of information from the ground, particularly in the neediest areas, it is impossible to know how many packages were successfully delivered to people in need and how many were not. All that the personnel delivering the packages can effectively judge is how many HDRs they dropped—an incomplete measure by any standard. Moreover, although 2.4 million HDRs were dropped over Afghanistan (at a unit cost of $4.30), each HDR is a single meal (although ostensibly incorporating a day's caloric allotment), and therefore the drops could have fed only a small fraction of the population for a limited period.

It is also difficult to assess whether the HDR drops achieved the goal of the information campaign, i.e., demonstrating to the population that the United States and its military bear no ill will. U.S. military personnel on the ground reported that the drops did generate a positive response among local populations.[13] Yet because the HDRs were only part of a far broader information effort to convey this view to the people of Afghanistan (and elsewhere), it is impossible to isolate the impact HDRs had on attitudes toward U.S. military action. Special Forces personnel returning from Afghanistan have stated that HDR drops, particularly those using containerized delivery systems (rather than being "flutter-dropped" as individual packets), generated good will among the Afghan communities within which they occurred.

---

[12] Interviews at the United Nations, April 23, 2003.

[13] Information provided by DoD personnel, October 2003.

Those actually involved in planning and implementing the drops had mixed feelings about them. Some thought them an effective and successful tool, arguing that HDRs were effective in OEF and fed some individuals who otherwise would not have had any access to food assistance. This assertion is difficult to substantiate, however, and certainly plenty of others doubted the usefulness of the drops.[14] The available data do not support any clear assessment one way or the other.

Civil Affairs During Combat Operations

During the fight against the Taliban in late 2001, civil-affairs forces played a role in the combat phase of the military operation. Elements of the 96th Civil Affairs Battalion, the sole active-duty Army civil-affairs unit, deployed to Afghanistan and conducted operations in coordination with U.S. Special Operations forces (SOFs) that were operating there. This was very different from the events of recent operations in the Balkans, where civil affairs did not enter the theater until the post-conflict phase. In Afghanistan, a wide variety of operations, including CMOs, were ongoing simultaneously. The goal of civil affairs during this period was to assist local supporters of coalition forces and to thus undertake projects that visibly indicated U.S. endorsement of the local political leadership. Civil-affairs personnel, working with other U.S. forces (non-SOF), were responsible for some of the initial liaisons with local leaders in several Afghan cities. Their efforts included the preliminary identification of possible assistance projects, although they were unable to begin implementing these projects immediately because they did not have ready access to funds (discussed in detail below).[15]

Given leeway by their superiors and following the example of some SOFs working in Afghanistan, some civil-affairs commanders decided to allow their teams to wear civilian clothes while conducting operations. These teams did not deny that they were U.S. soldiers,

---

[14] Interview with CENTCOM Commander General Franks, September 2002.

[15] Interviews with U.S. military personnel, October 2002.

but they did attempt to blend into the community to the extent possible. They also emphasized to Afghans that their mission was to provide assistance. Facial hair, some argued, helped them in their dealings with local leaders. The wearing of uniforms varied by region: Some teams stayed in uniform, others modified it slightly, and others wore civilian clothes at all times. Concerns about force protection, particularly given the significant exposure of the small civil-affairs teams, guided these decisions.[16] At the same time, the decisions planted seeds for confusion among Afghans when USAID, IO, and NGO assistance providers arrived wearing civilian clothes.

Planning for the CJCMOTF

The footprint and timeframe issues (noted above), combined with the lack of readily deployable civil-affairs units and CENTCOM's focus on the logistical elements of assistance, heavily shaped the structure of the CJCMOTF on the ground in Afghanistan. While civil-affairs and assistance efforts could, to some extent, be run out of CENTCOM, it became increasingly clear to planners that a structure in Afghanistan was necessary to help coordinate these activities and provide military support to the humanitarian activities of others. The CJCMOTF concept has been an element of joint and Army doctrine for some time but had never actually been deployed before OEF. Because this was the first deployment, the approach was not etched in stone, and planners had, in principle, a good deal of flexibility in structuring and deploying the CJCMOTF. In practice, the debate among CENTCOM and U.S. Army Forces Central Command (ARCENT) planners concerned whether assistance in Afghanistan would be primarily a question of logistics or one of traditional civil-affairs tasks. In the end, the logisticians won, in part due to the limited input of civil-affairs personnel. Thus, the CJCMOTF was planned with fairly little contribution from policy personnel responsible for issues of civil-military affairs.

---

[16] Ibid.

One aspect of this debate was whether assistance would be delivered on what was termed a "wholesale" or a "retail" basis.[17] The planners preferred the former, meaning that the primary U.S. military involvement in humanitarian relief operations was expected to be the establishment of humanitarian supply depots outside Afghanistan. These facilities would serve as resupply points for NGOs, foreign government donors, and IOs conducting humanitarian operations inside Afghanistan. The U.S. military might help coordinate theater-level logistical support for humanitarian operations, such as movement control and lift-requirements analysis, but they would not become involved in directly assessing humanitarian requirements or delivering aid within Afghanistan.[18] Early planning called for the CJCMOTF to be based in Dushanbe, Tajikistan, rather than Afghanistan itself.[19] Such an approach was consistent with the limited primary goals of OEF emphasizing a minimum U.S. footprint.

This logistics focus had significant implications for the structure of the CJCMOTF. First, it was not organized as a civil-affairs brigade or battalion, but rather was a composite of the 122nd Rear Operations Cell and the Army Reserve 377th Theater Support Command, along with personnel from the 352nd Civil Affairs Command, the 511th MP Company, and the 489th and 96th Civil Affairs Battalions.[20] Civil-affairs staff constituted a minority of the initial CJCMOTF staff. They were concentrated in a CMO staff cell within it (the civil-affairs staff assigned regionally throughout Afghanistan reported to the CJCMOTF, but they were not a part of its internal structure).[21]

ARCENT and CENTCOM officials believed that this organization was appropriate for what they expected to be largely a logistics

---

[17] Interview with a U.S. military planner, May 2002.

[18] Interview with a CMO planner, October 2002. Airdrops of HDRs were the primary exception to this policy. However, in this case, the exception proves the point.

[19] Interviews with U.S. military personnel, summer and fall 2002.

[20] Center of Excellence in Disaster Management and Humanitarian Assistance website, http://coe-dmha.org/inter_cjcmotf.htm, accessed March 28, 2003.

[21] Interviews with U.S. military personnel, November 2002.

mission, and indeed, such a mission was very much in line with their past experience and structures.[22] It should be noted, however, that even if planners had wanted to utilize a civil-affairs unit as the core of the CJCMOTF, it is unclear that they could have done so. The Army has only one active-duty civil-affairs battalion and none of the higher headquarters (brigades and groups) required to run a CJCMOTF. Therefore, it would have been a Reserve unit. DoD would have been hard-pressed to rapidly deploy the CJCMOTF with the full staffing needed, because mobilizing Reserve component units is a time-consuming process. Delaying the deployment of the CJCMOTF to this extent was not a viable option—putting a structure in place early was critical to ensuring that assistance efforts were rapidly and effectively implemented. Thus, the logistics focus may well have been as much a result of what was possible for an early deployment as a conscious decision on the part of CENTCOM and ARCENT leaders.

It is also worth noting that some believe this CJCMOTF structure was the result of a conscious desire by some in the DoD leadership to move away from the Balkans model of CMOs, where civil-affairs forces largely supported the efforts of civilian government agencies, primarily USAID, and depended on them for assistance priorities and funding.[23]

IOs and NGOs

A discussion of civil-military relations in the provision of assistance in Afghanistan must necessarily be broken into two components. The first is the relationship between military personnel and civilian personnel representing other USG agencies; the second is the relationship between the military and nongovernment (IO and NGO) civilian actors. These relationships are interdependent, but they are also very different in tenor and structure.

---

[22] Interviews with U.S. military personnel, fall 2002.

[23] Interviews with U.S. military personnel, November 2002.

From the UN perspective, once combat operations began, the reduced level of assistance that continued after the evacuation of internationals had to be still further curtailed. WFP deliveries continued to trickle in, mostly in the north, but local staff members came under heavy pressure from the Taliban. Contacts with their sponsoring organizations were sporadic, and they almost always took place in the presence of a Taliban monitor. Nevertheless, local staff remained a valuable source of information on the plight of needy populations.

Military and civilian actors had a strong mutual interest in exchanging information about the locations of food warehouses, other IO and NGO facilities and personnel, and food convoys to keep them from being targeted. Other items of joint concern were the movements of IDPs and security conditions throughout Afghanistan. The mechanism immediately available for this purpose was the UN Security Coordinator (UNSECOORD), the agency that handles security matters for the UN system, which met on a daily basis throughout the combat phase to exchange information about these matters. Since information from the U.S. government had to percolate to the U.S. Mission at the United Nations, to UNSECOORD, through the UN bureaucracy, and finally out to the field, the process was cumbersome and prone to delay.

The United Nations established a joint logistics center (JLC) in late September for managing aid delivery. The JLC, which initially operated out of Islamabad, was run by WFP. It served as an interagency center for coordination of logistics and transport for all the UN agencies involved in-theater. The activities of the JLC and other UN agencies were overseen by the UN regional coordinator, who was also responsible for the UN resident coordinators in neighboring states (Iran, Tajikistan, Turkmenistan, and Uzbekistan). The JLC served as the primary conduit for tracking aid deliveries down to the level of secondary and tertiary carriers, and this information was provided to CENTCOM through the WFP and OCHA liaisons. The JLC also took the lead for civil-military relations at the operational level between the United Nations and the military. This set the pattern for subsequent months. CJCMOTF staff looked to UN *logisticians* to "validate" humanitarian assistance decisions (such as deciding among CJCMOTF humanitarian assistance projects under consideration), rather than consulting with the actual humanitarian assistance *programmers* in the UN system. This weakened the efficacy of this civil-military link.

As the campaign against the Taliban gathered momentum in November, conditions improved to the point that humanitarian operations inside Afghanistan could be resumed on a piecemeal basis. Even before the fall of Kabul in mid-November, UNSECOORD was able to identify "permissive" areas where cross-border food deliveries could be conducted. Information provided by the coalition about threat conditions, areas contaminated by unexploded ordnance, and the location of distressed groups made it possible to accelerate the humanitarian response as Taliban resistance crumbled.

Aspects of the rhetoric surrounding the global "war on terror" and its Afghanistan component put many humanitarian NGOs on edge. British Prime Minister Tony Blair spoke of a "military-humanitarian coalition," and Secretary of State Colin Powell described NGOs as a "force multiplier, essential contributors to the United States' combat team."[24] Given the centrality of impartiality to professional civilian humanitarian aid organizations (particularly NGOs), employment of the term *humanitarian* by belligerents and the suggestion that humanitarian action was but one facet of a coordinated American-led effort generated great unease. This was not merely a theoretical concern; some NGO workers (both national and expatriate staff) believe that they came under pressure as a result of a perception on the part of local Afghans that they were aligned with foreign military actors.[25]

---

[24] Nicholas de Torrente, "The War on Terror's Challenge to Humanitarian Action," in *Humanitarian Exchange*, London: Overseas Development Institute, November 2002, available at http://www.odihpn.org/documents/humanitarianexchange022.pdf.

[25] Interviews with UN officials, April 23, 2003.

The OCHA interagency plan for continuing support to the Afghan people during and after the conflict was conceived by UN agencies and NGOs and envisioned a four-stage process:

- Evacuation of international staff (accomplished by 16 September).
- Post-evacuation, pre-military intervention.
- Military intervention.
- Post-intervention.

OCHA planners expected that the work of NGOs would be increasingly difficult to sustain and that support to vulnerable groups would disappear in the interregnum between international evacuation and the launch of the military air offensive.[26] This proved largely not to be the case. A subsequent plan (dated November 15) noted:

> The humanitarian situation in the weeks since the military intervention commenced has been marked by large scale displacement (40–70 percent of urban populations) and increased numbers of extremely vulnerable people. The volatile security environment has greatly eroded humanitarian space and hindered access to these groups. [However,]. . . national staff of agencies have continued to operate, but with highly restricted mobility, logistics, and communications capacity."[27] The plan went on to indicate that "within the next 30 days, the UN and its partners will endeavor to re-establish an international presence throughout Afghanistan in areas where security conditions allow.[28]

---

[26] United Nations Office for the Coordination of Humanitarian Assistance to Afghanistan, "Donor Alert: To Support an Inter-Agency Emergency Humanitarian Assistance Plan for Afghans in Afghanistan and Neighboring Countries (October 2001–March 2002)," September 27, 2001.

[27] United Nations Office for the Coordination of Humanitarian Assistance to Afghanistan, "30 Day Emergency Operational Assistance Plan for Afghanistan: 15 November–15 December 2001," November 15, 2001.

[28] Ibid.

IOs and NGOs began reintroducing their international staff to Afghanistan on a rolling basis, beginning in the north (where some NGO expatriate and national staff had remained), as the security situation allowed.[29]

NGO activities during the combat phase of operations in Afghanistan usually closely paralleled those of the United Nations. This occurred, in part, because many NGOs take their guidance on matters such as security and movements from the UNSECOORD offices in New York. This practice is not voluntary; it is often a requirement in order for the NGOs (particularly those funded by the United Nations) to acquire insurance for their personnel and equipment. The difficulties in communications and in determining "ground truth" in the many different regions within Afghanistan exacerbated the problems of coordinating efforts remotely (from evacuation sites in Peshawar, Islamabad, and Tashkent) and of making the difficult security decisions about returning to Afghanistan, where to return, with how many staff, and under what conditions. None of the field reports or interviews conducted with NGO personnel for this study mentioned close collaboration with coalition military forces. Although interviews with U.S. military personnel and UNSECOORD indicate that there was some degree of coordination, this was unknown to those working in the field. UN and NGO operators there were very sensitive about military vehicles being parked in front of their offices, for example, as they feared that this would lead Afghans to identify them as part of the military coalition. They preferred to keep operational-level interaction with the coalition to a minimum, and when it did occur, it was limited to issues such as security and contingency plans for evacuation and medical emergencies.[30]

Despite the challenges that OEF presented to humanitarian aid operations, IOs and NGOs worked throughout this difficult period. Efforts to help remedy three years of drought and to prepare for Afghanistan's forbidding winter helped prepare them for the contin-

---

[29] Interviews with UN officials, April 23, 2003.

[30] We thank George Devendorf of Mercy Corps for this point.

gency that OEF presented. The supply lines for this effort were exceedingly long, some running all the way to Latvia. Throughout November and December, security and winter weather were both limiting factors for NGO activities. Distributions through December varied by region. Food aid delivered into the country to provincial hubs (not necessarily delivered to villages) was estimated to satisfy from 80 percent to 150 percent of anticipated requirements across the north and northeast (where the drought was worst). In the west and central highlands region, deliveries through December satisfied from 40 percent to 80 percent of expected needs. By January 2002, Oxfam reported that large amounts of food had finally gotten into the country and that distribution was generally satisfactory.[31]

The movement of goods and materiel into the region by the international community, while complicated and requiring careful coordination, encountered fewer impediments than many had feared. Aid was able to flow into Afghanistan, and food and other aid stockpiles for the winter meant that the assistance effort was not starting from zero. The onward movement of goods and services and the coordination of efforts in-country did present serious challenges. Field reports from a variety of agencies noted the difficulties during this period of contacting indigenous staff working in Afghanistan. Even though expatriate international staff had relocated in many cases to the closest neighboring country in order to facilitate continued coordination and effort, it became nearly impossible to maintain regular communications channels during the war. Afghan NGOs and local staff of international aid organizations were under considerable physical threat throughout the air campaign because of their perceived association with military forces.

Despite the inherent difficulties of a wartime environment, local NGOs and local staff of international NGOs were able to cope with the combat operations surprisingly well. As was noted, the stockpiles created in anticipation of winter conditions had helped prepare the

---

[31] "Crisis in Afghanistan," Oxfam Update Humanitarian Situation, January 11, 2002, available at http://www.reliefweb.int/w/rwb.nsf/0/3bb1779af59e2f08c1256b44003a29fa?Open Document.

humanitarian assistance community and "system" for the problems associated with an unexpected war. The combination of fewer weather-related problems than expected, effective local partners, and a long-standing assistance community in the country and region helped ensure that the humanitarian response to the deepening crisis in Afghanistan did not falter during the combat operations of October 7 through December 5.

USAID

Deliberate and strategic engagements were undertaken by USAID/DCHA and the Department of State's Bureau of South Asian Affairs. On October 4, the same day that President Bush announced a $320 million assistance program, Assistant Secretary of State Christina Rocca re-declared a complex humanitarian disaster in Afghanistan for FY 2002. This triggered a multiagency assistance effort involving USAID (OFDA, Food for Peace [FFP], and the Office of Transition Initiatives [OTI]), the U.S. Department of Agriculture (USDA), the Centers for Disease Control and Prevention (CDC), and the Department of State (Bureau of Population, Refugees, and Migration [PRM], Humanitarian Demining Programs [HDP], and Bureau of International Narcotics and Law Enforcement Affairs [INL]).

USAID's plan during October 2001 was a five-pronged approach to mitigating the disaster. The five strategic goals were:

- To reduce death rates in Afghanistan.
- To minimize population movements (both IDPs and refugees).
- To lower and then stabilize food prices so that food in markets would be more accessible.
- To ensure that aid reached those for whom it was intended.
- To begin developmental relief projects in order to move beyond emergency relief to long-overdue reconstruction projects.[32]

---

[32] Ibid.

U.S. financial assistance during this period was significant. Assistance in FY 2001 totaled $184 million, and in FY 2002 it increased to $531.4 million, with significant growth in virtually every category of spending (see Table 5.1).[33]

The dramatic increase in assistance between FY 2001 and FY 2002 is, of course, to be expected. Clearly and understandably, the majority of the assistance was in the form of disaster-response assistance and food aid. The magnitude of the increase and the range of agencies contributing to the total amount, however, illustrate the interagency nature of the intra- and post-conflict efforts in Afghanistan.

Working mainly through WFP from Pakistan and the Central Asian states, USAID provided USG food aid to Afghanistan. USAID support for WFP's Afghan Humanitarian Assistance Program accounted for approximately 85 percent of the WFP food in transit during October 2001. USAID engagements in Afghanistan did not cease during the period of combat, but they were modified to reflect

Table 5.1
U.S. Government Assistance Related to Afghanistan, FY2001-2002
(in dollars)

USG Agency	FY 2001	FY 2002
USAID/OFDA	12,485,791	113,345,576
USAID/FFP	31,200,000	159,472,700
USAID/OTI	NA	24,348,951
USAID/DG	310,000	NA
State/HDP	2,800,000	7,000,000
State/PRM	31,088,659	137,715,401
State/INL	1,500,000	NA
USDA	104,300,000	38,651,516
DoD	NA	50,897,769
CDC	569,525	NA
Total USG assistance	184,253,975	531,431,913

---

[33] U.S. Agency for International Development, "Afghanistan—Complex Emergency," Situation Report No. 4 (FY 2003), March 13, 2003, available at http://www.usaid.gov/ofda/publications/situation_reports/FY2003/afghanistan_ce.

the changing security situation.[34] NGOs were funded to undertake rehabilitation of wells, sanitation, and agriculture infrastructure, as well as to provide primary health care.

A major problem for USAID and its partner organizations was the lack of security on the ground in Afghanistan, which prevented USAID from deploying its people into the country. When the security situation improved, an element of the DARTs deployed to Kabul. In the absence of an embassy during this period, and despite its own security restrictions, the DART became an important factor in coordinating on-the-ground humanitarian assistance activities (not least because of its communications and reach-back capabilities).

Civilian-Military Relations

The presence of NGO and IO representatives at CENTCOM headquarters was unprecedented. Although problems, as noted throughout this report, did arise in the course of the mission, the arrangement was successful overall. It increased the dialogue among all concerned, and it enabled exchanges of information, often at very high levels. The UN and NGO liaisons were able to translate the terminology and redlines of civilian humanitarian aid organizations to the military, and the military was able to explain its own terminology and procedures to the civilians. For example, when CENTCOM personnel noted that UN Situation Reports had identified a break in the food pipeline, the military considered responding with HDR drops to the areas affected. However, because UN and NGO liaisons were consulted on this decision, they were able to explain to CENTCOM that such breaks were not unusual and that the assistance agencies in place would be able to work around them. In a similar way, concerns in military circles about NGO reports of a

---

[34] Andrew Natsios, testimony before a Joint Hearing of the Subcommittee on Near Eastern and South Asian Affairs and the Subcommittee on International Operations and Terrorism, Committee on Foreign Relations, U.S. Senate, on "Afghanistan's Humanitarian Crisis," October 10, 2001.

dismal humanitarian situation were calmed by UN and NGO liaison explanations that while the situation was indeed difficult, such reports did not always accurately reflect conditions on the ground but were, rather, a mechanism for soliciting and maintaining financial and other support for the NGOs in question and/or the overall humanitarian effort.[35]

The presence of civilian liaisons from the UN, NGOs, and the U.S. government helped support the effort to minimize damage to civilian infrastructure, cultural and religious sites, and other important elements as the military plan was developed. Identifying where NGOs and IOs had their own facilities and also getting information from these groups, many of whom had had personnel in Afghanistan for years, on the location of critical Afghan sites that might need protection were important components of planning an effective campaign. In return, military personnel informed NGO and IO representatives of the locations of cluster bombs.[36]

This is not to say that the process always ran smoothly. NGOs and IOs believed that they provided more information than they received. Moreover, some feared that providing locations of their facilities to CENTCOM might lead the military to destroy them for fear that they could fall into Taliban hands.[37] Military personnel were frustrated by the NGOs' inability to provide reliable data on the location of aid and convoys, not recognizing that these generally involved contractor vehicles and were not always easy to track. Both groups found military and USG security classification rules particularly frustrating. There were times when military personnel could only hint at locations and times that civilians might want to avoid but could not provide clear guidance on specific dangers and risks. For instance, while U.S. forces tried to provide civilian de-miners with all the information they legally could, they were limited by classification concerns. Moreover, they could not provide information on how to

---

[35] Interviews with IO and NGO representatives, July 2002.

[36] Interviews with U.S. military personnel, fall 2002.

[37] Interviews with IO and NGO representatives, May 2002.

defuse U.S. mines.[38] Another problem was that the targeting computers could not directly accept no-strike grid coordinates. Instead, such information was included in the air tasking order's Special Instruction Notification, placing the onus on pilots.[39]

The informal coordination structures involved significant one-on-one discussions between IO and NGO personnel, including nearly monthly meetings with General Franks, on an *ad hoc* basis.[40] In addition, two formal structures were created to deconflict assistance activities: the Humanitarian Activities Coordination Council (HACC) and the Humanitarian Activities Working Group (HAWG).

The HACC met daily in the trailer of the CENTCOM policy team at the coalition village and included representatives from the UN agencies, InterAction, and CENTCOM. It was designed to provide a forum for resolving short-timeline crises. CENTCOM briefed participants on incidents and events in Afghanistan and also provided intelligence (at an unclassified level). The HACC became the forum for discussions of such issues as the wearing of civilian clothing by military personnel, treatment of captives, and HDR drops. Civilian representatives found the involvement of senior CENTCOM officials in the occasional meetings particularly useful. The HACC met monthly with the CENTCOM deputy commander, and participants reported that these meetings were very useful.[41]

Whereas the HACC was primarily a forum in which CENTCOM personnel could interact with NGO and IO representatives, the HAWG enabled the assistance providers to interact also with representatives of coalition military forces. These groups met daily in the early days of the campaign, but later the frequency of their meetings dropped to two or three times per week. The HAWG evolved into the primary forum for defining what various coalition

---

[38] Interviews with U.S. military personnel, November 2002.

[39] Ibid.

[40] Interviews with IO and NGO representatives, fall 2002.

[41] Ibid.

militaries were providing to support humanitarian operations, as contrasted to the crisis focus of the HACC. However, only five of the 20 countries that participated in HAWG meetings provided significant contributions to assistance efforts. The HAWG was a useful mechanism for encouraging non-U.S. coalition members to fulfill the requests of NGOs and IOs.[42]

Overall, the involvement of nonmilitary personnel at CENTCOM was a useful contribution to OEF. However, the benefits declined over time. The U.S. State Department and USAID withdrew their representatives from CENTCOM in early 2002, after the defeat of the Taliban led most activity to shift from Tampa to the field. Many in the NGO and IO/UN community thought such liaisons should be established in-theater (i.e., in Kabul) to improve the information flow. UN and NGO representatives were concerned that this would require them to leave as well, since the State Department and USAID had been the primary sponsors for their presence. Later, USAID provided representation to CENTCOM once again, but the State Department remained unrepresented. InterAction maintained staff at CENTCOM until July 2002, and various UN agencies maintained an intermittent presence until that time. After July 2002, however, there were no NGO or IO representatives in Tampa.[43]

The CENTCOM CJCMOTF was responsible for the broader deconfliction of air traffic. In principle, UNJLC was to consolidate all IO and NGO requests and send them through its liaison in Tampa to CENTCOM, which would then pass them on to the Combined Forces Air Component Command (CFACC). The process was frustrating, with military personnel complaining that they rarely got the information with sufficient notice (they requested 72 hours), while UNJLC complained that it was never told if flights were approved or denied.[44]

---

[42] Interviews with IO and NGO representatives, July 2002.

[43] Interviews with U.S. military personnel and with IO and NGO representatives, spring, summer, and fall 2002.

[44] Interview with U.S. Army Peacekeeping Institute, April 23, 2003.

The Islamabad CHLC remained a primary coordinating body for humanitarian flights into Afghanistan in the early stages of the campaign. The senior coalition air force controller in Qatar effectively controlled the airspace over Afghanistan, and the CJCMOTF in Tampa provided clearance for flights, but the CHLC had to keep track of the flights going into and out of Pakistan, the key staging area. UNJLC sent its consolidated air requests (received from throughout the international assistance community) to CENTCOM, which combined and deconflicted them, in part based on HAWG inputs, and sent them on to the field, including Islamabad. Sometimes UNJLC also provided them directly to the CHLC in Islamabad (perhaps because of the lack of response from CENTCOM). When the CHLC received information about planned humanitarian flights from UNJLC, it communicated that information to Prince Sultan Air Base, CENTCOM (in Tampa and Qatar), relevant embassy personnel, and U.S. forces in Afghanistan.[45]

Humanitarian flights had to be deconflicted from one another, as well as from the coalition air campaign. The CHLC requested 24 hours' notice of flight plans, and it reported that the process tended to go smoothly when this request was honored. However, the notice was not always available, and there was considerable confusion about what flights were going where and when. Three different UN agencies, as well as the ICRC, were independently sending aid flights into Afghanistan. UNJLC was responsible, as noted, for consolidating all requests and transmitting them to the coalition, but at times, various agencies passed their plans to the CHLC directly, so that UNJLC was not aware of them at all. E-mail became a primary mechanism for these communications. Similarly, NGOs were supposed to coordinate flights through UNJLC (and thus through CENTCOM), but these flight plans, too, sometimes went directly to the CHLC, particularly if the NGOs were unhappy at the scheduling and response they received from UNJLC. The resulting confusion sometimes led to very

---

[45] Interviews with U.S. military personnel, fall 2002.

short notice on flights. Coalition countries also varied in the degree to which they shared information with the CHLC regarding their humanitarian aid deliveries.[46]

The situation in Pakistan reflected the complications of air traffic deconfliction at other points in the process as well, and it certainly tracks with the situation at CENTCOM itself. Some of the problems of this process could perhaps have been averted if a regional air movement control center had been set up earlier (one was deployed in February 2002). A regional control center is responsible solely for coordinating and deconflicting flights into and out of the theater of operations and vicinity, and such a center would have taken the burden off the CJCMOTF and the CHLC. Apparently, it was not deployed sooner because it is not doctrinal for the Air Force to deploy such a structure, although one was very effectively used in the Balkans (and eventually in Afghanistan, as well).[47]

There were few foreign staff of IOs or NGOs in Afghanistan during fall 2001. Most had left the country during September or early October, before OEF started, although a small number remained or attempted to restart operations immediately in the wake of coalition military advances. Most of the civil-affairs personnel interviewed for this study believed that the civil-military relationship in the field during this period was excellent. There was a lot of cooperation and coordination with NGOs and IOs present, because all were focused on the task at hand, and interests were sufficiently similar that coordination was possible. Many soldiers observed that this cooperation decreased the further one got away from the field and toward headquarters locations.[48]

---

[46] Interviews with U.S. military personnel, October 2002.

[47] Interview with U.S. Army Peacekeeping Institute staff, May, 2003.

[48] Interviews with U.S. military personnel, October 2002.

Assessing CMOs During the Fight Against the Taliban

From the military's perspective, CMOs had an important effect during the effort to remove the Taliban from power in fall 2001. The presence of civil-affairs teams in various regions of Afghanistan supported effective working relationships with the local authorities and helped in addressing the most immediate problems in communities. These efforts generally built good will among the populace and helped fulfill the CENTCOM commander's intent of making sure the Afghan people understood that the war was not against them. The difficulty of initiating projects may have undermined this good will somewhat, since promised projects were delayed, but as discussed in the following chapter, once funds arrived, the projects began and their impact, from a military perspective, was rapid and far-reaching.

In addition to the direct effect of civil-affairs activities on the villages and towns, an important side benefit was their high public relations value, both in Afghanistan and beyond. Television, radio, and newspaper coverage of the military conducting humanitarian assistance work projected a positive image in the country and abroad of the military working to help the Afghan people.

However, many civilian aid providers, both within and outside the U.S. government, believed that frequent targeting errors that killed Afghan civilians undercut any headway made on humanitarian and reconstruction projects. "One strike negated 100 projects, and not just OHDACA [Overseas Humanitarian, Disaster, and Civic Aid]-funded projects, either," noted one USG observer.[49] The civil-affairs activity was seen by many civilian aid providers and observers as a self-serving exercise aimed at the home front and internationally, not at the Afghan audience, which was not served by the mass media channels that covered the effort. The reference points of the Afghan people were far more immediate.

---

[49] Interview with USAID personnel, February 2004.

CHAPTER SIX

Humanitarian Assistance and Reconstruction Efforts Between December 5, 2001, and June 1, 2002

Military Humanitarian-Type Activities

The CJCMOTF

U.S. military civil-affairs personnel were involved in a broad range of activities that supported humanitarian assistance and reconstruction. These included participation in planning at CENTCOM, coordination between military forces and IOs and NGOs, direct support to Special Forces teams throughout Afghanistan, and the coordination of specific assistance projects.

Chains of command were critically important. CENTCOM, in both Tampa and Qatar, had overall authority for OEF (under the guidance of the President and the Secretary of Defense). ARCENT was the component command responsible for Army operations. The forces that deployed belonged to a variety of other commands, such as the 377th Theater Support Command and the U.S. Army Civil Affairs and Psychological Operations Command (which is itself part of the Army Special Operations Command). For the duration of OEF, they reported to ARCENT and CENTCOM, as appropriate.

The CJCMOTF was established by CENTCOM at MacDill AFB in Tampa in October and was the structure responsible for coordination of assistance. This CJCMOTF was critically involved in the airlift support discussed in Chapter Five. In December, CJCMOTF elements began to deploy forward to Kabul, leaving behind in Tampa a small element to continue the coordination work begun there. This meant that until late summer 2002, when the Tampa part of the CJCMOTF was stood down and its personnel were dispersed to new assignments at CENTCOM, there were two CJCMOTF locations. Both CJCMOTF structures reported to COMCFLCC/ARCENT, General Paul Mikolashek, and composed one of the conventional task forces operating in Afghanistan, along with Task Force Mountain (formed by the 10th Mountain Division). The Kabul CJCMOTF was commanded by Brigadier General David Kratzer. It managed all the activities of all civil-affairs personnel in Afghanistan not assigned to SOF elements and was also supposed to coordinate the assistance efforts of other members of the military coalition in Afghanistan. It was tasked to do all of this while maintaining the relatively small footprint discussed previously.[1]

The CHLCs reported to the CJCMOTF through one of two CMOCs, either CMOC North, located at Karchi Khanabad airbase in Uzbekistan, or CMOC South, in Kabul.[2] Following the model of the first CHLC in Islamabad (i.e., as a CMOC under a different name), the CHLCs were deployed throughout Afghanistan to coordinate the provision of humanitarian-type assistance and to liaise with nonmilitary assistance providers. Located in Afghanistan's major cities, including Kabul, they were built on the basis of the units of the 96th Civil Affairs Battalion which initially deployed throughout the country. The CJCMOTF in Kabul approved CHLC assistance projects and other operations. It was the primary interlocutor with civilian assistance providers and Afghan citizens in the field.

The CJCMOTF deployed to Afghanistan while discussions about its structure and mission continued. As noted in Chapter Five, the logisticians had won the debate about the fundamental structure of the team, but its actual mission remained unclear. CJCMOTF personnel reported that the high-level guidance they received when deploying to Afghanistan encouraged them to "do things," rather than merely supporting (through site surveys, for example) and coordinating the efforts of others.[3] With this instruction, the CJCMOTF

---

[1] Conversation with U.S. Army personnel engaged in civil affairs, July 28, 2004.

[2] Ibid.

[3] Interviews with personnel from CENTCOM and the CJCMOTF, spring and fall 2002.

took its first steps toward becoming a direct provider of assistance rather than a logistics hub.[4]

The origins of the perceived directive to "do things" are complex. Certainly a good bit of it came at the direction of CENTCOM Commander General Tommy Franks, who saw visible activities as a critical imperative for the U.S. mission, contributing to the broad goals of OEF. But other factors were also involved. Although the directive seems to conflict with the logistics structure of the CJCMOTF, some believe that it reflected the lack of experience with civil-affairs activities on the part of the CJCMOTF's predominantly non–civil-affairs personnel. Another explanation is that it derived from the Combined Force Land Component Command (CFLCC) commander's emphasis on force protection and engendering local confidence, support, and good will toward the U.S. forces. The deployment of civil-affairs troops in support of Special Forces, again in part for force protection, may also have played a role in creating an atmosphere stressing more-tangible action and activity.[5]

The CJCMOTF was staffed by personnel from the 377th Theater Support Command and the 122nd Rear Operations Command, along with a small number of civil-affairs personnel. This configuration led to a highlighting of theater-level logistics instead of operational and tactical involvement in the delivery of humanitarian assistance.[6] This emphasis on logistics may have hampered the capacity for direct action, while reinforcing the perception that such action was a goal. Certainly it made it difficult to carry out the "retail" aspects of civil-military coordination and assistance that became the bulk of the CJCMOTF's activity.[7]

Many saw the logistics focus and the absence of significant numbers of civil-affairs personnel as reasons for lags in implementing some more-typical CMO activities, including developing a system to

---

[4] Interviews with U.S. military personnel, summer and fall 2002.

[5] Interviews with U.S. military personnel, spring 2002.

[6] Conversation with U.S. Army personnel engaged in civil affairs, July 28, 2004.

[7] Interviews with operational-level civil-affairs planners, May and September 2002.

assess humanitarian requirements, defining measures of effectiveness for CMO projects, and coordinating with other civilian USG agencies, IOs, and NGOs. Moreover, when more civil-affairs troops did move into Afghanistan, they found the CJCMOTF not fully prepared to support them, because the equipment brought in by the units that established the CJCMOTF was not what a civil-affairs team would have used. Communications and other expected necessary equipment were not in place, and assistance activities had no dedicated air assets, so civil-affairs personnel were required to use UN aircraft instead. This sometimes hampered resupply for forces in the field and was responsible for water shortages in Herat.[8]

Footprint constraints were another challenge for the CJCMOTF. Because of the decision to limit the number of military personnel in Afghanistan, relatively few civil-military liaison personnel were deployed. This made it difficult to maintain good communications between various forces and units—for instance, between civil-affairs elements within the conventional structure and SOF elements that performed similar, or related, missions. Moreover, there appeared to be no formal liaison arrangement between civil-affairs elements in Afghanistan and UN agencies or between other coalition civil-affairs elements and the CJCMOTF. Although there was a formal CJCMOTF liaison to ISAF civil-military cooperation (CIMIC), some personnel were not aware of this.[9] Such standing liaison arrangements are critical to efficient and effective coordination of civil-military operations in the theater.

As it turned out, the CJCMOTF staff began almost immediately to define projects that they could carry out or support, developing a database of 100 possibilities by February 2002. These projects included a variety of assistance efforts based on needs identified by the local communities, such as the need for schools. The CJCMOTF could not immediately implement the projects, however, because funding for them came from DoD's Overseas Humanitarian, Disas-

---

[8] Interviews with U.S. military personnel, November 2002.

[9] Interviews with operational-level civil-affairs planners, May and September 2002.

ter, and Civic Aid (OHDACA) appropriation. OHDACA was designed for activities that required some lead time, rather than for the kinds of quick-impact and fast-response projects the CJCMOTF developed and believed it was required to undertake. Although OSD released OHDACA funds and delegated decisionmaking authority to CENTCOM in February 2002, CJCMOTF staff were frustrated at the several weeks required for a process to be developed in the field to ensure that project coordination and approval met DoD policy and legal requirements. Sometimes the CJCMOTF staff even used their own money to jump-start activities. CJCMOTF insistence that the OHDACA process be streamlined ultimately led to a considerably reduced staffing process and improved disbursement time.

Another constraint on OHDACA disbursement was the result of a misunderstanding. Because projects over $300,000 had to be individually approved by OSD, many in the field believed that there was a $300,000 cap on OHDACA funding for individual projects.[10] Although OSD was actually quite interested in funding larger projects, CJCMOTF personnel were reluctant to forward them on, believing that they stood very little chance of approval.[11] This generated more friction with IO and NGO personnel, who wanted the military to undertake temporary infrastructure repairs to enable freedom of movement.

Overall, however, the OHDACA funding was a tremendously effective mechanism for enabling the CJCMOTF to support active assistance. It certainly supported military goals of demonstrating U.S. good will—direct assistance was far better than the HDR drops—and it helped a number of people (although the failure to establish measures of effectiveness and, indeed, the difficulty of doing so for such an effort make it difficult to provide precise judgments). However, despite its successes, there were concerns that the focus on direct assistance not only took away from traditional civil affairs activities, but also may have made them seem less necessary. For instance, if military

---

[10] Conversation with U.S. Army personnel engaged in civil affairs, July 28, 2004.

[11] Interviews with USG and U.S. military personnel, Fall 2002.

personnel can disburse funding directly, they have less incentive to coordinate effectively with civilian groups and agencies to ensure that the assistance is provided. Moreover, some NGO and IO representatives argued that the military efforts to provide assistance were shoddy, lacking the follow-through and systematic cohesion of more-effective and experienced civilian assistance efforts.

ISAF CIMIC

As the CJCMOTF was establishing itself in Kabul during early 2002, the UK-led International Security Assistance Force (ISAF) was deploying forces to stabilize Kabul. The British commanded ISAF from January to July 2002. One of the principal efforts in this period was CIMIC. The UK saw CIMIC as a critical and integral component of ISAF's mission and overtly identified force protection as a reason to prioritize CIMIC. Where the CJCMOTF was a largely independent task force in the capital city, operationally and geographically distinct from the U.S. combat element in Bagram, ISAF CIMIC appeared to be more closely integrated into overall ISAF peacekeeping operations.[12]

Unlike the CJCMOTF, ISAF CIMIC was able to disburse funds almost immediately after arriving in-theater. The UK CIMIC had a special arrangement with the UK Department for International Development (DFID), which reimbursed military assistance expenditures *ex post facto*. As a result, U.S. forces handed over some projects to ISAF for implementation in the early weeks of 2002. As part of its force-protection mission, ISAF rapidly launched small, quick-impact projects to create visible results that the population would attribute to the force, including building schools in time for the new school year and providing basic facilities. ISAF paid Afghans to do the work and provided a secure environment in which the projects could go forward. By July 2002, ISAF had carried out some 200 projects and had spent some $4 million in its operating area of Kabul.[13]

---

[12] Interviews with ISAF personnel in the United Kingdom, August and November 2002.

[13] Ibid.

CHLCs

CHLC assistance activities emphasized low-level infrastructure, such as schools, hospitals, and wells. Civil-affairs personnel also actively distributed supplies for schools and hospitals, having visited almost 60 schools and almost 40 hospitals by mid-July 2002.[14] CHLC staff got input from local authorities on what sorts of projects were needed, asked local contractors for cost estimates, and then decided which projects to fund. Reserve-component project evaluation teams were responsible for evaluating the work and comparing it with the provisions of the contract. Local firms often subcontracted with others for aspects of the work. U.S. personnel reported that Afghans who had been living in the West but had returned to Afghanistan were particularly helpful in facilitating programs and projects.[15]

This assistance demonstrated U.S. good will to the local populace. In fact, civil-affairs personnel often built close personal relationships with local officials. Regional governors, hearing about projects elsewhere in Afghanistan, would ask for such teams in their regions. Some relationships were so close that U.S. personnel lived with the local individuals in their homes or compounds.[16] The relationships varied from region to region. In Mazar-e-Sharif, for instance, Special Forces interfaced with the warlords, while the civil-affairs team focused on the new government representatives.[17] U.S. personnel believe that such ties may have helped them serve as interlocutors between the local leaders and the NGO/IO humanitarian assistance community as a whole, with Afghanistan's new civilian government, with civilian representatives of other governments, and even among the local leaders themselves.[18]

---

[14] Joseph Giordono, "GIs Show Afghan Orphans 'We're Here to Help,'" *European Stars and Stripes,* July 12, 2002.

[15] Interviews with U.S. military personnel, November 2002.

[16] Ibid.

[17] Ibid.

[18] Ibid.

Specific activities were different in each region. In Kunduz, the local CHLC focused on OHDACA-funded projects that the 96th Civil Affairs Battalion had set up.[19] These included building eight schools and one hospital wing and digging 12 wells. While funding was briefly paused, the CHLC carried out assessments of villages and developed maps suitable for sharing with other U.S. personnel.[20] Also in Kunduz, civil-affairs personnel coordinated with the International Organization for Migration (IOM) and local officials to develop a system for repatriation of refugees from Pakistan. The civil-affairs forces had limited transport and food to support this effort. (Lacking excess transport capacity, the U.S. military moved most of its humanitarian assistance on contracted civilian trucks.[21]) The civil-affairs role was almost exclusively one of coordination, identifying requirements, and keeping local leaders and civilian assistance providers up to speed on each other's activities and efforts.[22]

Military personnel saw CHLC activities around Deh Rawod as particularly successful. This region had been the setting for the tragic (and much publicized) accidental bombing of a wedding party by U.S. forces. Local residents were quite hostile to U.S. forces after this event, throwing rocks at U.S. personnel, for example. After civil-affairs troops supported the construction of a clinic and some wells in the region, however, local attitudes appeared to improve and the hostility dissipated. Other examples of effective assistance included the efforts of an Army Reserve dentist who reportedly contributed significantly to efforts to restructure Afghanistan's medical system in that area.[23]

By summer 2002, civil-affairs personnel in southern Afghanistan were overseeing reconstruction activities in more than 50 villages near

---

[19] The CHLC was taken over in March 2002 by the 489th Civil Affairs Battalion.

[20] Interviews with U.S. military personnel, November 2002.

[21] Ibid.

[22] Ibid.

[23] Ibid.

Kandahar.[24] Military personnel argued that many of their efforts focused on areas of Afghanistan where the NGO community was unable or unwilling to go. An example was provided by civil-affairs Sgt. Arthur C. Willis in a discussion with a reporter observing a delivery of construction material to a remote village. The trip took 50 minutes by Chinook helicopter, whereas it was an all-day drive from Kandahar, leading Willis to remark, "We get to go to places where they can't go, or won't go."[25] In Kabul, for instance, the CHLC sought to concentrate on areas outside the ISAF CIMIC area of responsibility and beyond the reach of the Kabul NGOs to avoid duplication of effort and to help mitigate civil-military tension.

At this stage, military resources that had initially been deployed to support combat missions were being pressed into service for assistance efforts. Military doctors reportedly treated more civilians than they did combatants.[26] Medical assistance included coalition military units as well as units from the United States. The Jordanian-built hospital in Mazar-e-Sharif treated about 106,000 civilians in the first year of the conflict, and the Korean hospital in Manas also treated many civilians. The CHLC in Mazar-e-Sharif was described as the only real CHLC, in the sense that it was the only one with a significant coalition presence, including civil-affairs personnel from the United States, Jordan, France, and Britain. The Jordanian hospital was supplemented by French control of the local airfield, British efforts to coordinate with a local university, and Uzbek forces under Abdurashid Dostum in the area. NGO representatives were critical of the hospital, however, arguing that it was in an urban area, while most of the need was in rural areas. They also said that the Jordanians were failing to train Afghans to take their place, thus making it unlikely that the facility would be maintained after the coalition left.

---

[24] James Scott, "Rebuilding a Country, One Village at a Time," *Charleston Post and Courier* (SC), July 14, 2002, p. 9.

[25] James Brooke, "U.S. Tasks in Afghan Desert: Hunt Taliban, Tote Plywood," *New York Times*, September 14, 2002, p. 1.

[26] Indira A.R. Lakshmanan, "Boredom Is Surgical Team's Ideal Battleground Scenario," *Boston Globe*, October 6, 2002, p. 16.

U.S. military personnel disagreed, noting that the hospital planners coordinated with local officials and with the main hospital in the area to ensure that it would meet long-term needs and sustainability requirements. (NGO/IO personnel often express concern that military civil-affairs personnel do not have a perspective beyond their immediate operational vicinity.[27])

CHLC personnel also complained about the initial slowness of OHDACA fund disbursement. They argued that an operational fund for assistance activities would have been helpful for supporting small-scale projects and bridging funding gaps. While the CHLCs could carry out other activities even without the funds, they found that their credibility with the local people, who continued to come to them with requests, was damaged. As with the CJCMOTF, CHLC personnel reported that, at times, funds for activities were generated from the in-theater personnel to support local needs.[28]

Another problem for the CHLCs was that the effort to coordinate with other organizations, support SOFs, and provide assistance, all while maintaining a light footprint, meant that there was not sufficient staff to do these jobs as well as they could have been done. In order to stay within the established force cap, many civil-affairs personnel were deployed to Afghanistan as individual augmentees.[29] Unfortunately, the existing system for calling up and deploying individual civil-affairs augmentees is not sufficiently sophisticated to ensure that the right personnel are provided to the staffs and units that require them. As a result, a significant proportion of the augmentees were deployed to units that did not need their particular expertise, while other units went without or waited an unnecessarily long time for such expertise.[30]

---

[27] Eric Schmitt, "In Afghanistan: What's Past and What's Still to Come," *New York Times*, October 13, 2002; interviews with NGO representatives, summer 2002.

[28] Interviews with U.S. military personnel, Fall 2002.

[29] Interview with a CMO planner, May 2002.

[30] Interview with an operational-level civil-affairs planner, May 2002.

Additionally, footprint restrictions led to the deployment of civil-affairs elements that were fractions of existing units, rather than entire units. Missions were generally assigned to a civil-affairs battalion or a portion thereof, and these structures lacked the personnel to furnish sufficient direct support teams to meet all of the reported needs, to provide CMO support to various other forces while managing humanitarian-type assistance projects, and to coordinate with other assistance providers. Moreover, civil-affairs elements were deployed to the theater without critical equipment and supplies. For example, augmentees provided by the 489th Civil Affairs Battalion to Task Force Mountain (10th Mountain Division) were unable to conduct effective coordination with NGOs because they were deployed without armored M988 Humvees, the only means by which they could travel from Kandahar Airport to the city center, where the NGOs were based.[31]

Coordination Among Military Forces and Personnel

There is nothing new about having multiple international military forces, all with different mandates and missions, in place and active in the same theater. That was the situation in Somalia, for example. However, the fact that the situation is not unprecedented does not make coordinating a variety of disparate military organizations and militaries any less difficult. In Afghanistan, the forces in question were ISAF, the multinational peacekeeping force in Kabul, and the coalition warfighting force, CJTF-180.

Afghanistan also presented the additional challenge of continuing combat operations even as relief, reconstruction, and stability assistance was actively ongoing. This may have been exacerbated by the deep involvement of U.S. forces in assistance and reconstruction, given their absence from the formal peacekeeping mission. The limited international participation in the military force contributed to perceptions of a strange division of labor between the United States and the rest of the international community.

---

[31] Interviews with USG and U.S. military personnel, spring, summer, and fall 2002.

Within the U.S. force, a good deal of friction developed in regard to the role of and authority over the CJCMOTF. While under CJTF-180, the command linkage ran directly from the commander of CJTF-180 to the commander of the CJCMOTF. CJCMOTF personnel believed that this structure was not always respected by the XVIII Airborne Corps staff, particularly its CMO principal staff officer (the CJ-9), whom they viewed as believing he could direct orders to the commander of the CJCMOTF. Some XVIII Airborne Corps staff seemed to see the CJCMOTF as an enlarged civil-affairs staff for the ground commander. CJCMOTF staff chafed at what seemed to them an undue amount of interference in their efforts.[32]

As a task force, however, the CJCMOTF's influence was limited. The CJCMOTF oversaw the CHLCs, coordinating their resupply and approving their project plans. CHLC staff, meanwhile, had their own regional operations in addition to supporting those of other military personnel active in their region. The CJCMOTF also served a coordinating role in the capital and became involved in some specific projects.[33] It coordinated extensively with ISAF and ISAF CIMIC. A CJCMOTF liaison team attended all ISAF meetings and kept up informal relations. Participants generally assessed relations between ISAF and CJTF-180 as quite good.[34]

Another coordination issue was the handoff of responsibility between various commands. Some of the logistics problems in transferring control of the CJCMOTF were discussed above. The CHLC teams, established by the 96th Civil Affairs Battalion (regular Army), reported good transfers. The first of these saw the 96th's CHLCs relieved in place by the 489th Civil Affairs Battalion (U.S. Army Reserve) in early spring 2002. The second rotation, in late fall 2002, brought in the 450th Civil Affairs Battalion, also a Reserve unit.[35]

---

[32] Conversation with U.S. Army personnel engaged in civil affairs, July 28, 2004.

[33] Interviews with U.S. military personnel, October 2002.

[34] Interviews with U.S. military and ISAF personnel, November 2002.

[35] Conversation with U.S. Army personnel engaged in civil affairs, July 28, 2004.

USAID's Role

With combat continuing in Afghanistan, December 2001 marked the beginning of a new and more complex period in terms of civilian assistance. While humanitarian needs continued, the emergency phase of that assistance was ending. On December 13, DoD conducted its final airdrop of HDRs following consultations with the United Nations and other humanitarian aid organizations. The bulk of food assistance was flowing into Afghanistan by truck from neighboring countries, under WFP auspices. At the same time, the security situation in Kabul was improving to the point that NGOs, IOs, and USAID/DART personnel were arriving to reopen offices or undertake their own assessments of assistance needs on the ground. USAID/DART members were traveling in and out of Kabul from the DART base in Islamabad (the Central Asia DART was closed during this period).

Slowly, the mindset within the civilian assistance community was shifting from purely humanitarian assistance to include reconstruction and nation-building programs as well. USAID/OTI began funding a nationwide radio network and provided funding to the UNDP Fund for Government Operations, enabling the Afghan Interim Authority (AIA) to begin reconstituting a government structure in Kabul. This made for a more complex coordination process because NGO, IO, and USG civilian activities now joined the coalition military assistance activities on the ground in Afghanistan. The re-emerging government authorities were also demanding a role in the assistance process.

On December 18, 2001, the U.S. Embassy formally reopened. The embassy included a USAID Mission and, later, Ambassador William Taylor as U.S. Special Representative for Donor Assistance. On January 21, 2002, Japan hosted the International Conference on Reconstruction Assistance to Afghanistan (ICRAA), where donors pledged $4.5 billion in economic aid. They committed to providing $1.8 billion of that in 2002, the U.S. share being $296 million.

While slow to get started, the international presence in Afghanistan was beginning to take shape, at least in Kabul. In early March

2002, the UN Secretary General proposed the establishment of the UN Assistance Mission in Afghanistan (UNAMA). Built on the foundation of UNSMA (which had long been in existence) and presumably combining the capacities of the UN agencies, UNAMA appeared in the context of a very dangerous and dynamic security environment. That limited all of its activities, diplomatic as well as assistance. Direct coordination between the U.S. military, NGOs, and the United Nations initially proved difficult. At the same time, the NGOs and IOs demanded that the coalition provide an enabling security environment for them to undertake their assistance activities in a recognized humanitarian space. In April 2002, the Islamabad-based DART moved to Kabul to coordinate with the humanitarian relief community and assess the situation.

Planning began for the June 10–16 Loya Jirga to determine the two-year transitional government that would run Afghanistan until elections could be held in 2004. This focused the international community's attention on the need to strengthen the authority and legitimacy of the AIA, mandated at the Bonn Conference in December 2001 and under the leadership of Hamid Karzai. The need for the coalition to back regional leaders in order to gain their support during the combat phase in Afghanistan had the unintended consequence of weakening the hand of the Karzai government in Kabul. Schools and wells restored by coalition forces in areas under the control of warlords reinforced the warlords' prestige and stature.

IO and NGO Activities

When humanitarian activities picked up inside Afghanistan, the need for coordination among civilian humanitarian aid providers and coalition forces in the field became paramount. Yet field-level contacts raised some of the most acute concerns about the violation of humanitarian space. These concerns were reflected in guidance for the relationship between UN and coalition forces issued by the UN regional coordinator in Islamabad, who had the lead for UN efforts in Afghanistan. He was conservative in his approach and proposed limited association with coalition "combatant" forces to protect UN neutrality and freedom of action. This guidance governed interaction with representatives of the coalition until summer 2002.

On March 28, 2002, UNSCR 1401 established UNAMA to undertake tasks specified in the Bonn Agreement, which identified the transitional governmental structures for Afghanistan. To simplify structures, UNAMA absorbed the UNSMA and UNOCHA. UNAMA was composed of two "pillars," one for political affairs and the other for relief, recovery, and reconstruction. Since ISAF had already been deployed in December and UNAMA's mandate did not include responsibility for those peace-keeping forces, the UNAMA mission initially fell under the aegis of the UN Department for Political Affairs (DPA).[36]

Planning for the mission was conducted by a New York-based integrated mission task force (IMTF) comprising various key UN agencies involved in Afghanistan. While the IMTF produced discussion papers and proposals for UNAMA, the real impetus for structuring the mission came not from UN Headquarters but rather from the future UNAMA SRSG, Lakhdar Brahimi. In particular, Brahimi felt that UNAMA should be an assistance mission to the Afghan Transitional Authority under Karzai, rather than a transitional administration (e.g., as was the case in Kosovo and East Timor). Additionally, he insisted that UN agencies operating in Afghanistan be integrated under his authority as SRSG. The IMTF planning process incorporated both political concerns and the views of practitioners into the deliberations and served as an effective mechanism for keeping the UN Secretary General and other interested entities in the UN system informed. Once UNAMA began operations, the IMTF was transformed into a management support group consisting of the Department of Political Affairs, the Department of Peacekeeping

---

[36] This was the largest political mission ever conducted, and DPA had to rely on the Department for Peacekeeping Operations (DPKO) for logistical support. The United Nations subsequently determined that such "large" political missions should be run by DPKO. The transition to DPKO took place in November 2002.

Operations, OCHA, the UN Development Program, and UNHCR which met on a weekly basis.

While coalition forces continued to engage in combat operations during this period, both civilians and soldiers were active in providing humanitarian relief and initial reconstruction assistance. Civilian aid providers were therefore keenly interested in maintaining a distinction between their activities and those of combatant forces, so it was vitally important for the humanitarian relief community to operate independent convoys and airlift capability. This was essential to maintain access to needy populations in contested areas and for the safety of the aid providers.

The implementation of quick-impact projects and related reconstruction activities by coalition forces also raised a number of issues. These projects usually involved repairing schools and health clinics and similar small-scale efforts—precisely the realm where civilian aid providers believed they had a comparative advantage and a larger scale of activities. The sustainability of these projects was a frequent concern. Generally, civilian agencies would have preferred to see the military's unique engineering resources used to repair basic infrastructure, such as roads, bridges, power generation, and water supply systems. That would have allowed the civilian agencies to do their own work more effectively while also presumably building a sense of good will toward the military among the population by allowing the restart of commerce and employment. However, civilian aid providers were unable to operate in many areas of the country (e.g., Paktia, Paktika, Khost, and Gardez provinces), and they acknowledged the desirability of military assistance in these places. Since there were more than enough small-scale project needs to go around, more-effective coordination might have made this a less salient concern.

Coordination, however, was a complicated and vexing matter in an environment where the UN and NGO community feared that association with one of the combatant forces would imperil its perceived neutrality, increase the security threat, and limit its subsequent ability to accomplish missions over the longer term. Including a coalition representative as a routine participant in meetings of the OCHA-organized emergency task force that included IOs and NGOs was therefore unacceptable. During the early stages, UN agencies were also confused by the lack of apparent purpose of the military's reconstruction efforts and by the multiple forms military assistance came in, from SOFs, to civil-affairs personnel, to USAID. In spite of the confusion, however, there was no reticence about coordinating with USAID on a close and continuing basis, because IOs and NGOs viewed USAID as being distinct from the U.S. military.

Another barrier to effective coordination was the miniscule size of the military's reconstruction effort ($4 million) compared with the broader civilian effort ($1.2 billion). Thus, the return gained from the military effort expended was not always evident. The relatively small potential impact of the military activities, combined with the difficulties generated with civilian providers, led some in the NGO and IO community to question whether military humanitarian-type activities were worth the cost.

In sum, the mechanisms that the humanitarian assistance community found to be acceptable varied according to the proximity of the coordination mechanism to the fighting. The pragmatic need to deconflict the delivery of assistance from combat activity was satisfied through UNSECOORD and UNJLC and the establishment of temporary liaisons at CENTCOM headquarters. Although there were misgivings about the latter *ad hoc* mechanism, security concerns prevailed—as long as the interaction was discrete and low-profile. It was generally concluded that this liaison role was highly beneficial and worth replicating in the future. At the operational level in Afghanistan, however, a permanent or standing means of coordination was rejected by the IOs and NGOs in favor of a purely *ad hoc* approach. The overriding concern of these organizations was maintaining the perception by the local population that international civilian actors were autonomous and independent from the combatants.

Civilian-Military Relations

Within the U.S. government, working relationships went through not only traditional interagency structures, but also the innovation of liaisons at CENTCOM and unstructured cooperation in the field. In Washington, the usual tensions of interagency coordination significantly delayed the development of an integrated political-military plan for Afghanistan. The Clinton administration's interagency coordination structure for complex contingency operations (CCOs), outlined in 1997 in Presidential Decision Directive (PDD) 56, was not renewed or replaced by the Bush administration, and this made such coordination more difficult.[37] Furthermore, there was insufficient time to develop a coordinated interagency plan given the early start of the U.S.-led attack on the Taliban government and its rapid collapse.

In Afghanistan, representatives of USAID were initially skeptical of CJCMOTF and CHLC assistance projects. Over time, however, they became accustomed to coordination with military efforts. One of the main reasons for this change was the fact that military assistance was initially the only USG assistance being actively provided in Afghanistan, since USAID was unable to get personnel and funds into the field. Although OHDACA money did not become available until several weeks after deployment, USAID funds took even longer to arrive in-theater. Moreover, USAID staff operated under a series of constraints. First, the USAID personnel were initially deployed to Afghanistan on 45-day rotations, making it difficult to build relationships.[38] Second, security requirements imposed by the State Department made it extremely difficult for USAID staff to travel outside of Kabul. This was a product of both the lack of adequate security for these personnel due to the conflict situation and the absence of a mechanism by which the USG could guarantee their security. USAID staff fall within the State Department's sphere of responsibility, and the State Department lacked the organic assets to ensure their safety when traveling outside of Kabul. DoD, which had the capability to provide such security, did not have the organizational responsi-

---

[37] For more on PDD-56, see William P. Hamblett and Jerry G. Kline, "Interagency Cooperation: PDD 56 and Complex Contingency Operations," *Joint Force Quarterly*, spring 2000.

[38] Two-year rotation staff arrived in May and June 2002.

bility to do so. While these organizations were seeking ways to nego-
tiate *ad hoc* arrangements that would enable DoD to help assure
USAID staff safety, USAID personnel could not effectively oversee
and fund projects directly.

Instead, the CJCMOTF and CHLC staff communicated and
coordinated with USAID personnel, making sure that USAID saw
proposals under consideration and could confirm that they met government goals. This open and collaborative process made USAID
comfortable with the military taking on a large part of the burden
that USAID, at that time, could not assume. Although USAID did
not have formal authority to approve OHDACA projects, it appreci-
ated having the opportunity to provide input. When USAID did take
steps to limit activities, as when it called for a blanket ban on projects
in Mazar-e-Sharif, civil-affairs personnel cooperated.[39]

Eventually, USAID personnel were able to increase their capacity for movement throughout Afghanistan, enabling staff to more
effectively disburse assistance. (However, some diplomatic security
restrictions that make it far easier for DoD personnel to travel than
for USAID staff to do so remain in place to this day.) Relations with
military personnel remained cordial, and coordination was effective.
USAID personnel occasionally stayed with CHLC personnel when
traveling to the field, and some projects were co-sponsored by the
military and USAID. USAID's efforts were most flexible and effective
when USAID connected with civil-affairs teams for movement. All in
all, this relationship can be termed one of the critical successes of the
Afghanistan effort.[40]

There were difficulties in some relationships with other civilian
USG agencies and military forces. The CIA carried out a variety of
activities in Afghanistan, including the provision of humanitarian-
type assistance, with minimal coordination with military forces (or,
indeed, with other civilian USG representatives), and its involvement
often caused considerable confusion among both Afghans and coali-

---

[39] Interviews with U.S. government personnel, November 2002.

[40] Interviews with U.S. military personnel, November 2002.

tion personnel.[41] In addition, some U.S. agencies had no way to contact U.S. military personnel. Normally, the U.S. diplomatic mission would be responsible for ensuring that all civilian government agencies could interface effectively with the U.S. military in a given country. In this case, however, limited resources precluded this from being effectively carried out. Thus, the CDC, which had personnel in Afghanistan, reported that it believed U.S. forces saw it as just another NGO rather than as an agency of the U.S. government. NGOs argued that they had no suitable mechanism for communicating with U.S. and coalition military forces, and information exchanges regarding activities and plans that were possible in principle did not take place in practice.[42]

Relations with NGOs and IOs presented an entirely different model and set of challenges. Structures for integrating NGO and IO representatives into planning and coordination at CENTCOM in Tampa were both revolutionary and quite effective, suggesting a new template for such interaction. In Islamabad, too, while problems of logistical coordination arose among the many groups seeking to get aid into Afghanistan, relations were on the whole effective and cordial, although they varied significantly. In Kabul, where some of the NGO field headquarters, as well as ISAF and the CJCMOTF, were located, some of the gains of CENTCOM and Islamabad seemed to have been lost in that relationships were combative and difficult. Out in the countryside and in other towns and cities, relationships were excellent in some cases and almost nonexistent in others. Personnel who participated reported that it often depended on the individuals involved and, indeed, that relationships often changed along with individuals.[43]

One problem for everyone was the poor information flow between the field and various headquarters. For the military, the sheer number of structures created problems. CENTCOM policy planners,

---

[41] Ibid.

[42] Interview with a CDC official, August 2002.

[43] Interviews with U.S. military and NGO personnel, Fall 2002.

CJTF-180, the CJCMOTF, the CJCMOTF's separate planning organization at Tampa, and ARCENT were all involved at some level, and inefficient information flow was a problem for all of them. For example, the UN liaisons in Tampa were in principle expected to use CENTCOM mechanisms to communicate with their field headquarters in Afghanistan. They complained that this system lost or delayed many messages, some of which never got to Kabul. The problem was broader than the logistics of communicating through CENTCOM. Military and civilian personnel found that decisions were made in Tampa but were not passed to the field in time for action to be taken on them. Moreover, UN and NGO representatives often complained that their representatives in the field did not respond to requests for status reports for days, if they responded at all.[44]

The State Department's security restrictions on the travel of USAID personnel may have contributed to the tensions between military and NGO personnel. In past operations, USAID staff served as interlocutors between the military and NGOs, limiting direct contact between them and smoothing coordination and deconfliction. With limited ability to travel, USAID staff were unable to serve in that role until the restrictions were lifted. The direct contact between groups that were not particularly used to interacting may have contributed to the tension between them.

In theory, a number of formal structures were in place for coordination between NGOs, IOs, and coalition military personnel. From the perspective of military forces, the CJCMOTF had the mission of overall coordination of assistance for Afghanistan, and the CHLCs in key cities throughout the country had as one of their missions the development and maintenance of relationships with the NGO and IO community working in their vicinity, as well as ensuring that everyone involved could provide humanitarian assistance to the local populace. The CJCMOTF managed its coordination role in part by hosting weekly meetings at its compound, to which a variety of NGOs and IOs were invited. Although a number of IOs and

[44] Ibid.

NGOs regularly participated in these meetings, overall attendance was generally low and sporadic.[45] From the perspective of at least some in the NGO community, the CJCMOTF meeting was just one more meeting among many that laid claim to their time. Moreover, the security requirements for entering U.S. military facilities created strong disincentives for some NGO personnel. Some felt that these sessions were not particularly useful and thus not a priority. Additionally, some civilian officials reported feeling uncomfortable about entering a military compound and being around heavily armed soldiers.

Others had a more ideological opposition to the idea of the CJCMOTF—or the military more broadly—coordinating humanitarian assistance. Some saw these meetings as efforts by the military to extract information or even intelligence from the civilians, rather than to deconflict efforts and approaches, the stated goal of the CJCMOTF. The meetings were also perceived as a way for the military to seek to convince civilians that military activities were beneficial. The approach preferred by the United Nations and associated NGOs was to invite the coalition to send a representative on a case-by-case basis to their meetings when it perceived a need to do so. These organizations saw UNJLC (or UN operational agencies) as the predominant coordinating body for the delivery of humanitarian assistance.[46]

Generally speaking, military personnel interviewed for this study agreed with parts of this assessment. They confirmed that one aspect of interacting with NGOs and IOs was to gather data with which to better assess "ground truth," a particularly challenging effort given the small footprint of coalition military forces. However, they also believed that coordination was critically important and saw their role as the primary one for ensuring that coordination. Many military personnel reported a good relationship with UNJLC, but they did not

---

[45] Interviews with U.S. military personnel, summer and fall 2002.

[46] Interviews with CENTCOM and CJCMOTF personnel and NGO and IO representatives in Washington, Tampa, and Kabul, September–November 2002.

see it as the governing body for their own assistance efforts. There were no formal liaisons between military and civilian personnel in the field for the military coalition (ISAF did have such formal liaisons, as discussed below), and the meetings were the primary means for information-sharing.[47]

As noted, the relationships between regional CHLCs and the NGOs and IOs operating near them (in some cases dozens of NGOs and IOs, in others relatively few) depended almost entirely on the individuals in place at each location. Military personnel tended to report better relationships with former military personnel now working for the NGOs, but there were no hard and fast rules. In some regions, such as Kandahar, where military operations continued somewhat longer, tensions with some groups were high, although relations with others were excellent. In Paktia, military representatives reported almost no contact with NGO personnel. In other places, such as Bamian and Kunduz, relations were better, and civil-affairs personnel even attended some NGO and IO meetings to discuss needs, resources, and assessments (in Kunduz, this attendance was significantly limited, however). Under those circumstances, there was even effective handoff of projects from the CHLCs to NGOs and IOs.[48]

Civilian Attitudes Toward Military Humanitarian Assistance and the Issue of Uniforms

At the heart of tensions between military forces and civilians providing assistance were some very basic differences about the appropriateness of military efforts in this area and the directions in which such efforts, if they were undertaken, should be channeled. While it is impossible to speak of monolithic NGO and IO views or opinions, given the heterogeneity of these organizations, the civilian nongovernmental assistance community shares a number of common concerns about military assistance provision efforts. The first and

---

[47] Ibid.

[48] Ibid.

most fundamental divide might seem a mere semantic issue, but it goes to the crux of the difference between military, governmental, and nongovernmental assistance provision. The U.S. military consistently refers to its assistance efforts as *humanitarian*. NGO and IO personnel take issue with this use of the term, as discussed in Chapter Two.

Ongoing combat operations also raised serious NGO and IO concerns about relations with the military. In Afghanistan, while CIMIC and other ISAF elements were operating under a UN-endorsed peacekeeping mandate, OEF forces implementing humanitarian-type assistance projects had no mandate to provide this sort of assistance. This was a significant factor for the NGO community, one that led some organizations to avoid or limit contact with OEF forces.

NGO representatives also argued that through much of the first year of OEF, the military's efforts to build schools, hospitals, and wells were a relative waste of capabilities. Military assistance was expensive, had higher overhead than civilian efforts did, and was inefficient. The CJCMOTF and its CHLCs, with almost 200 soldiers, spent about $8 million in OHDACA projects, while the IOM obligated approximately $11 million with 11 expatriate staff.[49] They often argue that NGO and IO providers get more bang for the U.S. taxpayer buck than the military does.[50] In addition, NGOs argue that the military's inexperience in conducting assistance projects has numerous implications. In Afghanistan, they said, CHLCs made promises that were not fulfilled and raised hopes unfairly by looking at

---

[49] This is, of course, subject to debate. Military personnel point out that the assistance they provide goes directly to the people helped, rather than being spent on salaries and administrative costs, as is the case with NGO assistance. However, military salaries and infrastructure also cost money over and above the costs of the assistance, and the military indeed may have less of the know-how and experience needed to be efficient in assistance provision on the individual scale. (Interviews with U.S. military and NGO personnel, Fall 2002.)

[50] Civil-affairs troops dispute this assertion, noting that their efforts ran the full spectrum, from identification, planning, and contracting to execution and delivery, unlike NGOs and IOs, which often only identified and made grants. One civil-affairs officer noted that the dollar-for-dollar comparison touted was not an "apples-to-apples comparison."

dozens of projects before selecting only one or two.[51] They complained that military personnel inexperienced with contractors and
the local government made critical mistakes that hampered the assistance efforts of others. NGO and IO personnel assert that military
personnel expect to leave an area quickly, so they have less incentive
to make sure the projects they carry out can be sustained into the future—and indeed, the projects often prove unsustainable. Finally,
some NGO representatives expressed concern that accepting military
assistance may be seen as evidence of collaboration by local people, a
possibly dangerous situation for them should the balance of power
shift after coalition military forces leave. Thus, NGO representatives
contended that the long-term stability of the country would be pro-
moted most effectively if the military, instead of funding and
carrying out its own assistance efforts, took on major repair and construction projects to give the country a functioning infrastructure,
focusing on projects that are outside the capabilities of all but a few
NGOs, and providing a security umbrella.[52]

Military personnel have tended to dismiss the NGO concerns,
arguing that the assistance they provide does help people in the same
way as that provided by civilians. They also have their own complaints about working with NGOs and point out that many NGOs
have political and social agendas which they try to advance through
aid efforts. Military personnel highlight the complicated review processes for U.S. military assistance (for example, efforts to make sure
that the schools they assisted in Afghanistan were those on UNICEF's
priority list), and they argue that far from being expensive, their assistance efforts are relatively cheap compared with those of civilian
groups. They respond to NGO suggestions that the military should
focus on projects where it has more capability than others in the field
by noting the fact that the existence of the capabilities does not mean
that they are available for use in this way. Military engineers, however

---

[51] Military personnel also noted that the Afghans may have had trouble separating assessments from promises to implement projects. (Interviews with U.S. military personnel,
November 2002.)

[52] Interviews with U.S. military personnel and IO and NGO representatives, Fall 2002.

capable they are, were sent to Afghanistan to perform or support a warfighting mission, not to provide assistance, and they did not have the time and resources to take on these additional duties easily. Where and when possible, military personnel said, they would certainly devote engineering capabilities to assistance efforts, but only when this was in line with the broader priorities of the combat mission.

This debate summarizes the differences between military assistance providers and NGOs and IOs, a critical source of the tension between them. Military personnel see assistance as a component of the overall operation. For them, it is a means to an end, and the priorities of assistance efforts must be weighed against other priorities for the broader mission. For some NGOs and IOs, on the other hand, assistance *is* the mission.[53]

Many NGOs and IOs see another acceptable—even requisite—area for military involvement as the provision of a secure environment for NGOs and IOs that provide actual assistance. This is a complicated issue, feeding into another critical concern for NGOs operating in environments like that in Afghanistan, where military personnel are involved in combat as well as assistance missions. While there is a wide range of attitudes among NGOs, there is broad agreement that a clear line must be drawn between civilian organizations and military forces and that everyone should be able to distinguish between the two. As noted above, the fear that NGO personnel might be mistaken for military forces causes tremendous concern, which was brought clearly to light by the debate over the decision by some civil-affairs personnel to wear civilian clothes while conducting assistance-related tasks.

As discussed earlier, some civil-affairs personnel engaged in unconventional warfare operations in Afghanistan wore civilian clothing for force-protection reasons. These personnel reported that they were open about their status as soldiers to the Afghans they interacted with but did not want to be easily identifiable from a distance—com-

---

[53] Interviews with U.S. military personnel and IO and NGO representatives, Fall 2002.

manders feared that these personnel would become targets for Taliban or al Qaeda forces. In other areas, they chose to grow beards and wear civilian clothing in an effort to establish better relationships with local leaders. In still others, they avoided uniforms because local NGOs and IOs would interact with them only if they were in civilian clothes.[54]

The attitudes of NGOs in the field on this issue varied. According to some military observers, those outside Kabul did not seem particularly affected by whether local civil-affairs forces wore uniforms or not. These military sources also reported that Afghans had few concerns about this issue, although it might imply that they did not differentiate between the military and civilian assistance providers—precisely what NGO representatives feared.[55] NGOs disagree with this assessment. While there was a general understanding and acceptance of the military desire to win hearts and minds, many civilian aid providers believed their ability to perform their humanitarian mission was placed in real jeopardy by U.S. Army civil-affairs officers (and others, including U.S. and UK Special Operations units in the south) dispensing assistance while wearing civilian clothing. In Kabul, Tampa, and Washington, the uniform issue became increasingly important as IO and NGO personnel feared that U.S. soldiers in civilian clothes carrying out assistance activities greatly increased the risk that their own people would be mistaken for soldiers and thus be attacked by hostile forces. They were also concerned about the precedent this created for future operations.[56]

UN representatives had no reservations about approaching the CJCMOTF commander on this issue, and the NGO community went through OCHA to request that the UN Secretary General express his concerns to the United States. OCHA prepared a position paper, which the Secretary General provided to Ambassador

---

[54] Interviews with U.S. military personnel, Fall 2002.

[55] James Brooke, "Pentagon Tells Troops in Afghanistan: Shape Up and Dress Right," *New York Times*, September 12, 2002.

[56] Interviews with U.S. military personnel and IO and NGO representatives, Fall 2002.

Negroponte at the U.S. Mission to the United Nations.[57] NGO actions culminated in an April 2, 2002, letter from the heads of 16 major relief NGOs based in the United States. Working through InterAction, these groups wrote to U.S. National Security Advisor Condoleezza Rice, expressing "concern over U.S. military personnel conducting humanitarian activity wearing civilian clothes" and thus putting civilian aid workers at heightened risk.[58] On April 19, CENTCOM announced that military personnel would have to be clearly identifiable as such by their clothing and would wear at least some easily seen component of their uniform.[59] The time that elapsed between the time this issue was first raised and the time that the USG and DoD addressed it created a great deal of resentment in the NGO community.

While this issue was apparently successfully resolved, the conflict over it greatly increased tension between the U.S. military and NGOs. It continues to be raised by some NGO representatives as an example of military intransigence and lack of recognition of NGO needs, thus justifying limited contact with and distrust of coalition military personnel.[60] Perhaps more important, the uniform issue reflects the critical question of security and how it can best be assured in a conflict environment. Many IO and NGO humanitarian workers see clear differentiation of roles as integral to their own security, and the fact that U.S. forces remain engaged in combat amplifies these concerns. Many in the NGO community fear that for all the military's efforts to build trust among the local population through its assistance efforts, the Afghan people may not remain friendly to U.S. forces for the long term. Insofar as the NGOs plan to continue working in Afghanistan, they want to establish and maintain as clear a differentiation between themselves and military personnel as they

---

[57] Interviews with UN personnel, April 23, 2003.

[58] "Humanitarian Leaders Ask White House to Review Policy Allowing American Soldiers to Conduct Humanitarian Relief Programs in Civ," InterAction news release, April 2, 2002, available at http://www.interaction.org/newswire/detail.php?id=411.

[59] "U.S. Troops Working Relief to Modify Clothing," *Washington Post*, April 21, 2002.

[60] Interviews with U.S. military personnel and IO and NGO representatives, Fall 2002.

can. One NGO official put it thus: "When there is a backlash against the Americans, we want a clear definition between us and them." The difficulty of doing this when military forces also conduct assistance efforts was clearly highlighted by the uniform debate in Afghanistan.[61] In Afghanistan, some of this actually affected relations of the NGO and IO representatives not only with military forces, but also with USAID, as that organization's close relationship with the CJCMOTF and CHLCs tainted it to NGOs and IOs. While this may seem a strange notion given that USAID is a government agency and thus presumably is occupied with carrying out the same mission as is the U.S. military, the perception of USAID as an "honest broker" is worth noting.[62] The desire to draw a clear distinction between civilian nongovernmental assistance providers and military personnel may also have been a factor in the decision of some NGO personnel to avoid CJCMOTF and CHLC meetings, as traveling to and entering the facilities and compounds of these organizations might be seen as alignment with them.[63] For this and other reasons, some NGOs even have policies of "noncollaboration" with the military. Such groups not only resent the use of terms like *humanitarian* to refer to military assistance, they also protest the description of efforts to deconflict civilian and military assistance as *coordination*. However, it should be noted that even among these groups, there is a general acceptance of the need for some level of communication as long as everyone remains active, particularly for such things as flights and air traffic that cannot be successfully managed without some sort of contact.[64]

Differentiation between civilian and military assistance providers is not the only security issue that arose in Afghanistan. One traditional aspect of the military role in assistance is the creation of a

---

[61] Robert Fisk, "Return to Afghanistan: Americans Begin to Suffer Grim and Bloody Backlash," *The Independent* (London), August 14, 2002.

[62] Interviews with NGO personnel, November 2002.

[63] Ibid.

[64] Ibid.

"secure environment" in which civilian agencies can provide assistance to the populace. While some NGOs believe the military can best assure this environment by staying away from assistance activities, others argue that in a conflict situation, only combatant forces can provide security. Moreover, some point out that under the Geneva Conventions, occupying forces are obligated to help ensure that humanitarian assistance can be delivered, in part by providing security. The coalition force has argued that it is not, in fact, an occupying power in Afghanistan, since there is a new government in place, and therefore the coalition is not under this obligation. Thus, while security will be provided when and where the mission calls for it, it is not a separate requirement in and of itself.[65]

Given the experience in the Balkans, many had expected that the military would focus on providing a secure environment that enabled humanitarian activities, doing some surveys but not carrying out assistance projects. The fact that the CJCMOTF and CHLCs were, in fact, quite actively involved in assistance provision in Afghanistan is seen by many NGOs as a dangerous new development, particularly as it appears to be a possible template for future operations.

Civilian Relationships with ISAF CIMIC

The discussion of coordination mechanisms in Afghanistan is incomplete without a brief look at the experience of ISAF CIMIC in the same conflict. As already noted, ISAF was a separate military force, unrelated to the coalition and carrying out a UN-mandated peacekeeping mission in Kabul. ISAF was under British command from January to July 2002, when Turkey assumed command.[66] Both the British and Turkish forces saw CIMIC as a critical component of ISAF's mission.

---

[65] Interviews with U.S. military and NGO personnel, spring and fall 2002.

[66] Turkey commanded ISAF for a six-month period, followed by a six-month period of joint German and Dutch command. NATO then assumed command of ISAF.

In addition to its faster disbursement of funds, ISAF CIMIC contrasted sharply with the CJCMOTF in the relationship it built with IO and NGO personnel in Kabul. This was mainly the result of a UN Security Council mandate and the fact that ISAF was a peacekeeping, rather than a warfighting, force. Whereas the CJCMOTF was seen as a part of the military coalition, and thus part of the combatant force, ISAF clearly had a peacekeeping mission. ISAF had a civilian liaison from DFID in place to help advise the commander on civil-military issues, it maintained excellent lines of communication with the United Nations and various NGOs, and it assisted the United Nations with transport or aid and supplies whenever it had spare capacity. ISAF also kept databases on possible assistance projects that were generally assessed as the most comprehensive ones available and were thus used by IOs and NGOs as well as military personnel.[67]

Tension between military assistance providers and representatives of nongovernmental civilian agencies whose role is the provision of humanitarian assistance have been common throughout the history of such operations and to some extent must be seen as a permanent part of the landscape. That said, the specific problems and challenges posed by each operation should be considered as both sides strive to make the relationship a smoother and more effective one. The recognition that some problems may be endemic should not be a reason to avoid efforts to mitigate and, if possible, to eliminate them.

---

[67] Interviews with ISAF and NGO personnel in the United Kingdom and Kabul, Fall 2002.

CHAPTER SEVEN

Conclusion: Issues and Recommendations

The experience of civil-military relations in the delivery of humanitarian assistance in Afghanistan represents a major evolution in a continuing post–Cold War trend. Humanitarian assistance has become a challenging process in which development and security goals are pursued by many actors in concert and in conflict during CCOs.[1] The very nature of the war on terror has pushed the military into sectors that until recent times have not been its major concern, e.g., direct provision of humanitarian and humanitarian-type assistance in the midst of ongoing combat. The assistance itself is not novel, but the circumstances and motivations that lie behind it are. Moreover, the decision as to whether the benefits of military assistance provision outweigh the costs lies in the end with the U.S. Congress. While it is likely that military humanitarian assistance activities will be more proscribed in some situations, it is also almost certain that Congress will continue to fund such activities in many cases. Thus, unavoidable tensions between the military and the NGO and IO assistance community can be expected to recur.

Above all, the war on terror is the principal point of departure. In this war unlike any other the United States has been engaged in, the potential for failure flows not only from poorly executed military plans, but also from an inability to see assistance as a part of the con-

---

[1] Barbara J. Singleton, *A British Agencies Afghanistan Group Briefing Paper on the Development of Joint Regional Teams in Afghanistan*, London: Refugee Council, January 2003, p. 5.

tinuum from combat to post-conflict development and reconstruction.

Recommendations for USG Interagency Cooperation

Political-Military Planning

Circumstances surrounding the Afghanistan military action did not allow for much pre-execution planning and cooperation. Things moved too quickly, so that in effect, plans followed implementation. While policy was being debated, provisional policies were already being executed on the ground, and evolving policy discussions in Washington were rarely in synch with the dynamic realities in Afghanistan. This is not unusual—similar problems have arisen in other crises in remote locations. However, the Afghanistan experience highlights some possible solutions to this continuing problem.

Future success in such operations requires first of all a planning process that focuses on the strategic end-state and the means of execution. Only part of this is battlefield-related. The fundamental question concerns where the USG wants to be in terms of political and strategic outcomes when the combat stops and the role of humanitarian and other assistance in achieving this. The Afghanistan experience reveals that the lack of detailed pre-combat planning did not harm the immediate military outcome, but it did slow progress toward the political end-state. It also contributed to a view of assistance largely in terms of military objectives.

Lessons from this experience highlight the need for military and political planners to include each other's objectives as they prepare for such operations. Specifically:

- Military planners must evaluate the possible political consequences of various activities. In the case of Afghanistan, the HDR missions, the wearing of civilian clothes by soldiers, and even the use of the term *humanitarian assistance* to describe aspects of the CMOs created difficulties with the civilian nongovernmental humanitarian assistance community—and may even have hampered the attainment of other USG goals.

    – Guidance must be clearly defined (as should mission and mandates) and communicated effectively—to forces, within the USG, and, if possible, to other assistance providers.

- Clear chain-of-command relationships regarding CMO activities must be established.

    – At some point, there will be a transition from a military-controlled combat operation to an indigenous and/or internationally directed assistance process, although the combat phase may be protracted. This requires institutionalized time limits for military assistance and institutionalized mechanisms for transferring assistance projects to civilians.

- Each step of the planning process must address the classic "winning the war but losing the peace" conflict between combat objectives and postwar outcomes, or operational versus strategic thinking.

    – The military's potential need for support from regional leaders and militia forces during the combat phase of the operation must be recognized.

    – This need must also be balanced against the need to support strong central authority to ensure unity and security as a failed state is rebuilt.

    – It is necessary to maintain public security and the rule of law immediately in the aftermath of the combat phase of an operation.

An integrated political-military planning process that includes explicitly the role of assistance in achieving both the military and the political end-states must precede future interventions involving the use of military forces in any capacity. This process should address the following issues:

- The role of the military in providing humanitarian and humanitarian-type assistance during and after the combat phase of the operation. An effective examination of this issue should include:

  - A clear definition of the CMO mission that is integrated into the "commander's intent."
  - An assessment of the implications of that military mission for nonmilitary assistance providers and the integration into planning of mechanisms for mitigating problems.

- The short-term vs. long-term implications of assistance, i.e., the tradeoffs between quick-impact and developmentally sound projects and how these fit into the overall objectives of the operation. Critical aspects include:

  - An assessment of the appropriate role for USAID, NGOs, and IOs along the short- to long-term continuum.
  - Definition of the requirements of these organizations (e.g., security, neutrality) and how they affect the conduct of the overall operation.

- The mandate for humanitarian and humanitarian-type assistance. The presence or absence of an international mandate that addresses this sort of activity has a critical impact. We recommend that:

  - The U.S. government, in securing legitimating authority for *ad hoc* coalitions or other efforts to conduct military actions, seek to ensure that this authority includes language that explicitly addresses the need to conduct humanitarian operations as resources permit, allowing international organizations and others to cooperate with combat forces in the delivery of such assistance. If such a mandate is not possible, planners must understand and adjust for the impact on the "legitimacy" of military involvement in humanitarian and other assistance operations and also must consider the impact on the ability of UN organizations to undertake assistance operations.

- The impact of different mandates and corporate cultures on the assistance mission. Understanding that different assistance providers (USG, foreign governments, IOs, NGOs) have different approaches can help define ways to integrate their efforts into a complete plan.

Although the planning within the U.S. government regarding assistance seemed initially to follow implementation, the relationship between DoD and USAID worked well. This was in part because of the individual personalities involved and their shared experience—a number of the key USAID personnel had a military background. While that is an obvious plus for effective planning, it cannot be relied on for future contingencies and is insufficient from an institutional perspective. The USG must approach planning for assistance activities as a form of joint civil military operation. In Afghanistan, the military demonstrated convincingly the value of integrated, multiservice combat operations. In the same manner, the USG needs to better integrate USAID, the State Department, and DoD in the development and implementation of the overall political-military plan. We recommend consideration of new structures, perhaps modeled on the Federal Emergency Management Agency (FEMA), that can provide an interagency framework for assistance planning and coordination and for mobilizing the appropriate resources of other USG agencies.

We have not made a recommendation concerning the involvement of NGOs and IOs in the planning process. The experience in Afghanistan demonstrated the value of having IOs and NGOs present at CENTCOM headquarters for information-sharing and coordination. We do not believe, however, that integration of foreign and non-USG organizations into the USG planning process should be institutionalized. There are circumstances under which the involvement of such actors may be beneficial, but these circumstances will vary significantly on a case-by-case basis. However, USAID and the State Department's Bureau of Population, Refugees and Migration should actively consult the United Nations and other IOs and NGOs to ensure their input into the USG's planning process.

A Secure Enabling Environment for Humanitarian Assistance

The Afghanistan experience underscored the need for civilian and military operators to address the question of security. The traditional military response to IO and NGO requirements for an immediate and guaranteed security environment is that it is not the mission of U.S. forces to be the "cop on every corner." However, the lack of a secure environment limits, and may prevent, the deployment and effectiveness of civilian assistance providers. That, in turn, increases the burden on the military to provide assistance, straining its deployed force structure and capabilities and exacerbating tension with the civilian assistance community.

In Afghanistan, the fact that the U.S. military provided humanitarian-type assistance and engaged in combat operations but did not participate in the maintenance of a secure environment created a situation in which NGOs and others were expected to collaborate with combat coalition forces in assistance efforts, even though the combat coalition did not help provide security for those efforts. The success of ISAF in Kabul and the continued absence of a secure environment throughout much of the rest of the country suggests that the United States might have been better advised to address the public security needs of the country at an earlier stage and to have included the establishment of a secure environment in the mission of the U.S. and coalition forces.

We recommend that the USG begin to develop a strengthened and better-integrated capacity—both civilian and military—to address the public-order and rule-of-law aspects of establishing a secure environment in societies emerging from conflict.[2] Public security should be a component of the military's mission in the immediate aftermath of high-intensity combat operations, and this objective

---

[2] Robert Perito, "Establishing the Rule of Law in Iraq," *United States Institute of Peace Special Report 104*, April 2003, pp. 11–12.

should be recognized and incorporated into international mandates and USG planning. The U.S. military should not be the sole or even the principal provider of long-term public security in these societies, and parallel efforts should be made to improve the capacity of both civil agencies and other international actors to contribute. However, in most cases where U.S. forces are centrally engaged in the high-intensity combat phase, it will not be practical to leave the subsequent public security task solely to other civil and international actors.

Providing Assistance Under Combat Conditions

The conflict in Afghanistan is not the first situation in which the United States has faced the challenge of providing assistance under combat conditions. Such efforts in Afghanistan were complicated, however, by the presence of two international forces with different mandates within the same theater. Earlier operations, such as that in Somalia, showed even more starkly how problematic this situation can be. In Afghanistan, U.S. military forces were conducting combat operations and did not have an international peacekeeping mandate. Moreover, the mandates they did have did not cover the provision of humanitarian and humanitarian-type assistance. ISAF had an international peacekeeping mandate, but it was limited to the city of Kabul.

The U.S. and coalition military force was seen as a combatant by NGOs, IOs, and the local populace. This created a fundamentally different environment for USAID's bureaucratic structure of DART/OFDA, OTI, and USAID Mission to adapt to. We recommend the following, should similar operations arise in the future:

- The USG should seek to obtain an international mandate that covers the provision of humanitarian assistance and encourages coordination of effort, as noted above.

- The operational implications of multiple mandates and missions for CMOs and related assistance activities should be considered. CMOs may be used to support military operations, enhance force protection, win hearts and minds, or rebuild nations.

These missions are fraught with potential contradictions, however, and there are major differences in the way CMOs relate to nonmilitary assistance providers and to local inhabitants in areas of combat.

- DoD should establish a civil-affairs unit in the active component that can form the core of a CJCMOTF on very short notice. In practice, this would likely require the creation of a regular civil-affairs brigade or civil-affairs group headquarters within a U.S. Army Special Operations command.

- Rapid-disbursing, results-oriented assistance programs should be developed involving both military and civilian assistance providers, along with a mechanism for determining quick-impact vs. developmental projects. DoD's OHDACA and USAID's OTI represent the types of programs that can be valuable models for such programs. We recommend, however, that DoD and USAID examine how these might be improved—for example, by simplifying and streamlining their disbursement and approval process.

- The DART's role and capacities should be integrated with the U.S. military. This USAID mechanism is a proven vehicle for rapid deployment, needs assessment, and facilitation of humanitarian assistance in complex emergencies. While liaison officers from the UK equivalent, DFID, are embedded in UK military units and swing into action as part of those units, the DART does not have the same relationship with the U.S. military. We recommend that DoD and USAID examine the UK experience to see how DARTs might relate more closely to military assistance operations in the emergency-response phase.

- DoD and USAID should reach an understanding on the role of the DART as the interlocutor or coordination mechanism with NGOs and IOs. To succeed in this, DARTs will need physical access, freedom of movement, and credibility in that role. In addition, the State Department and USAID will need to examine whether security restrictions during combat and in the transition from combat operations prevent DARTs from playing that role.

Even in the combat stage of operations, civilian and military actors must begin planning a transitional mechanism for handling assistance in the gray period between the combat and post-combat phases. We recommend that consideration be given to naming a single person who could function as a coordinator for humanitarian and humanitarian-type assistance programs in a particular theater of operations. Ideally, this individual should be someone who could influence the assistance programs of foreign and international organizations as well. At a minimum, he or she should be able to coordinate U.S. civilian and military assistance programs, especially as the United States moves into the reconstruction and development phase of an operation.

Recommendations for Interaction with IOs and NGOs

If planning with NGOs and IOs is not possible, developing coordination mechanisms is the next best thing. Terminology is important from the perspective of NGO mandates and corporate cultures. For many NGOs, *coordination* is simply a way to exchange information— they do not want to create the perception of an integrated approach. We recommend that the USG acknowledge this to encourage the involvement of the largest number of key actors.

- **At the strategic level.** In the Afghanistan conflict, the CENTCOM mechanism for involving liaisons from NGOs and IOs resulted in unprecedented cooperation at the strategic level. These liaisons provide a good model for future operations, and we recommend further institutionalization of this process.

  We also recommend care with the use of terminology, particularly the reference to a variety of activities as *humanitarian*. While it is legitimate for a word to have different meanings for different groups and in different circumstances, the USG has an

interest in preserving a clear distinction between NGOs and
military providers of humanitarian-type assistance. Careful
use of terminology can help avoid confusion on the part of aid
recipients and others.

- **At the field level.** Because ongoing combat in Afghanistan precluded formal coordination at early stages, *ad hoc* mechanisms
evolved over time. NGOs and IOs in the field, however, were
reluctant to coordinate with a force regarded as a combatant.
Since this situation may recur in similar operations in the future,
we recommend using USAID as the formal coordinator with the
NGO/IO community. That arrangement would mitigate the
burden on the military and could help alleviate the sense of
competition that can result from different groups undertaking
similar activities in the assistance area. It could also help reduce
IO/NGO concerns about the compromised neutrality that
results from contact with one of the parties to a conflict.

    We also recommend that U.S. military personnel providing
humanitarian-type assistance wear uniforms to help clarify the
distinction between them and civilian aid providers. We recognize that there may be situations in which it is unsafe for military personnel to function in a given environment while in uniform. We recommend that in those situations, U.S. military
forces refrain from carrying out humanitarian-type missions and
that others (NGOs, civilian USG personnel) be responsible for
assistance provision. If U.S. military forces are the only ones
capable of providing assistance in a high-threat situation, the
need for a clear distinction disappears and the wearing of a uniform becomes less crucial.

- **Information flow.** The Afghanistan experience reinforced the
need for an information-management strategy and an infrastructure for coordinating information flows from the various groups
involved in humanitarian assistance. We recommend a thorough
assessment of the Afghanistan Information Management System
(AIMS) and the Department of State's Humanitarian Informa-

tion Unit (HIU) as the first step in putting together a formal system recognized by all players (government and nongovernment alike), with full interoperability across different databases. An important element in this process will be dealing with classified information. At the CENTCOM level, workarounds were used to deal with the problem concerning Afghanistan. This presented a greater challenge in the field.

In the Afghanistan crisis, as in previous humanitarian emergencies, a field-level humanitarian operations center that NGOs and IOs felt comfortable attending would have proven a valuable mechanism for coordinating logistical and security issues among civilian and military actors.[3] The CJCMOTF tried to perform this function, but its ability to do so was limited by the nature of the continuing conflict environment. The security restrictions placed on USAID personnel, specifically DARTs, became a particularly debilitating hurdle in this new environment. Their civilian intermediary role would have been extremely useful for facilitating communication between the military and humanitarian aid organizations. Unfortunately, there was no effective equivalent of a working humanitarian operations center in Afghanistan during this period.

We recommend that a regional air movement control center be created as a first step toward the provision of an effective information-sharing mechanism for civilian and military actors. This center would deal with information-sharing on targeting issues and how those issues might affect nonmilitary humanitarian assistance activities as well as NGO and IO assets in the field. The center could subsequently provide a basis for other forms of information-sharing such as assistance activities (perhaps through a common project database).

---

[3] William J. Garvelink, USAID Senior Deputy Assistant Administrator for Democracy, Conflict, and Humanitarian Assistance, "Humanitarian Assistance Following Military Operations: Overcoming Barriers," testimony before the Committee on Government Reform, Subcommittee on National Security, Emerging Threats, and International Relations, U.S. House of Representatives, May 13, 2003, available at http://www.usaid.gov/press/speeches/2003/ty030513.html.

Best intentions to work together notwithstanding, it is clear that in future operations, as in the past, there will be no agreement about whether parties are coordinating their activities or simply sharing information about activities they will undertake based solely on their respective mandates and internal policy direction. Disagreement regarding this question must be seen as an inherent element of CCOs.

Recommendations for Turning Lessons Learned into Lessons Applied

The experience in Afghanistan, despite its significant operational success, revealed a weakness in internalizing and applying relevant lessons learned from similar complex humanitarian emergencies. There is a requirement within DoD and USAID for institutionalizing the lessons and incorporating them in planning for and conducting future operations. We recommend that the Office of Foreign Disaster Assistance (OFDA) and USAID Policy and Program Coordination (AID/PPC) play that role for USAID. The National Defense University (NDU), the National Foreign Affairs Training Center (NFATC), and USIP could play a similar role for the USG interagency process as a whole.[4]

- **NGO and IO doctrine development.** A better USG lessons-learned process is only one part of the challenge. A similar effort should be undertaken to encourage the IOs and NGOs to become more focused on the development of a doctrine for humanitarian engagement. Afghanistan demonstrated that there is a need for closer coordination among NGOs, building on areas of common interest. Institutionally, it would be difficult for IOs and NGOs to work directly with the U.S. military in the devel-

---

[4] The Center of Excellence in Disaster Management and Humanitarian Assistance in Hawaii has done some innovative work, including reviews of doctrine and training, to facilitate better civil-military cooperation within government and between government and NGOs. Its site can be viewed at http://coe-dmha.org/index.htm.

opment of doctrine as well as in certain types of training. Therefore, we recommend that an outside group (for instance, USIP
working with the Pearson Peacekeeping Institute in Canada)
provide the venue for such an effort to (1) explore how to define
humanitarian space in the context of a global war on terror
where NGOs are largely and increasingly reliant on governments—some of whom may be combatants--for funding; and
(2) develop a framework for establishing measures of effectiveness to determine the success or failure of approaches to providing humanitarian assistance.

- **A joint doctrine for assistance.** Afghanistan validated the doctrine of joint operations among the U.S. military services. The
  military has internalized this lesson far better than has the civilian side of the USG. In the same way that the Goldwater-
  Nichols Act forced the concept of joint operations on the military, a similar outside push may be necessary within the Execu-
  tive branch to develop an integrated doctrine for conducting
  complex operations, including those undertaken in connection
  with combat operations.

  - **Integrated civilian-military planning.** PDD-56 articulated a
    policy for managing CCOs through an NSC-centered coor-
    dination mechanism. But even if PDD-56 had remained in
    force, its principles might not have applied in the case of Af-
    ghanistan, because it states that "unless otherwise directed,
    this PDD does not apply to . . . military operations con-
    ducted in defense of U.S. citizens, territory, or property, in-
    cluding counter-terrorism and hostage-rescue operations and
    international armed conflict."[5] An NSC-centered coordina-
    tion mechanism should be developed in light of the Afghani-
    stan experience to provide a more relevant basis for inter-

---

[5] *The Clinton Administration's Policy on Managing Complex Contingency Operations: Presidential Decision Directive May 1997*, PDD-56 White Paper, available at http://clinton2.nara.
gov/WH/EOP/NSC/html/documents/NSCDoc2.html.

agency coordination of CCOs, including those undertaken as part of combat operations, that would apply to future situations in the war on terror.

— **"Reserve" civilian capacity.** The military has successfully mobilized Reserve and National Guard elements for CMOs in Afghanistan, and the civilian side must develop a similar structured approach to creating a "reserve" capacity for humanitarian and other assistance efforts. Part of the slowness on the civilian side in responding to emergencies is attributable to the lack of large staffs and readily available equipment to conduct expeditionary operations.[6] One way to begin to address this mismatch between missions and available human resources is to draw on retired USAID and State Department officers with experience either in the region or in similar circumstances elsewhere. Assigning responsibility in emergencies is always done on the fly, with little ability to match specific requirements—which can normally be planned for in advance of the crisis—against specific individuals who are kept on standby. To ensure that evolving lessons are incorporated into practice, the designated cadre should be invited to participate with serving officials in a regular series of joint humanitarian-crisis exercises.

- **Integrating CMO/assistance strategies into military doctrine.** The military also must integrate CMO/assistance strategies into doctrinal development. The Afghanistan experience was clearly different from other recent interventions in that the U.S. military humanitarian-type assistance provision was not specifically governed by international mandate. The military's assistance mandate was constantly evolving in an environment that placed increasing demands on the force structure to "do nation-building." The question that must be addressed doctrinally is whether the Afghan experience is unique or the wave of the fu-

---

[6] Hamblet and Kline, p. 93.

ture in terms of military interventions with complex humanitarian crisis dimensions. If this is the wave of the future, then the CJCMOTF, CHLC, and provisional reconstruction team (PRT) structures must be carefully examined to determine their applicability to operationalizing as a new doctrine. Although the PRT experience is largely outside the time frame of this study, the security and assistance environment of that period provided the inspiration for this approach.

- **Guidelines for conduct of complex emergencies.** Finally, there is an unanswered question about the role of civil-military guidelines in the conduct of complex humanitarian emergencies as both a doctrinal tool and a training process. This could be an important aspect of interactions among the military, USAID, NGOs, and IOs. The act of developing such guidelines—an important and necessary next step in light of the Afghanistan experience—will encourage the cooperative environment necessary for undertaking successful assistance operations in the future. If the "You fight the way you train" motto can be applied to the assistance arena, exercising the guidelines is a necessary element in minimizing operational problems when confronting the challenges of delivering assistance in complex situations like that in Afghanistan.

Despite the need for efforts to achieve greater understanding, we must be realistic in our expectations. Even assuming the best of intentions on the part of all sides, the result will not be the creation of a well-oiled machine in which civilian and military elements work in perfect harmony to provide assistance to people in need. There will always be differing mandates and different corporate cultures, as well as different human and financial capabilities. Doctrine and training alone cannot change this. Doctrine and training can, however, help the various actors better understand each other's roles and capabilities and can thus enable them to be more effective when working in the same theater.

International Involvement in Afghanistan

This appendix provides additional historical information on issues relevant to this study. However, it is by no means intended to be an inclusive rendition of Afghanistan's complicated modern history.

International involvement in Afghanistan preceding and following the Taliban takeover represented five different perspectives:

- That of countries who supported the Taliban and recognized the new government.
- That of countries with regional interests and relations with antiregime warlords and regional leaders.
- That of countries with global interests (e.g., the United States and Russia).
- That of the United Nations, with its conflict mediation and humanitarian activities inside Afghanistan.
- That of NGOs that for security reasons usually operated from Pakistan in support of Afghan refugees.

Only three countries officially recognized the Islamic Emirate of Afghanistan—Pakistan, Saudi Arabia, and the United Arab Emirates (UAE). The rest of the international community, including most Muslim states, either denounced its aberrant form of Islam or condemned its violations of human rights. Pakistani and Saudi support were particularly significant.[1]

---

[1] Rashid, *Taliban*, p. 17.

Pakistan's Involvement in Afghanistan

The history of Pakistani involvement in Afghanistan reflects both Pakistan's regional political and security interests and connections between militant tribal and Islamic groups in both countries. According to Pakistani journalist Ahmed Rashid, throughout the 1980s, as the Soviets unsuccessfully sought to control Afghanistan, the fundamentalist Jamiat-e Ulema-i Islam (JUI) built a support base in Pakistan among Durrani Pashtuns living in Baluchistan and Northwest Frontier province.[2] From this base of support, the JUI opened *madrasas* (religious schools) and undertook relief work among Afghan refugees from southern Afghanistan and Kandahar who remained in Pakistan after Kabul fell to the mujahidin in 1992.[3] Many of the Durrani Pashtuns bought into the JUI's strict interpretation of Islam and became the core of the Taliban, a term with roots in the word *talib,* which means *student* in Arabic. When the Taliban took over in Afghanistan, it repaid its debt to the JUI by turning over camps inside the country to the JUI, which used them to train recruits for the conflicts under way in Kashmir, Chechnya, and the former Yugoslavia, among others.[4]

If the ISI and the government of Pakistan were ignoring the emergence of the JUI and the Taliban, criminal business interests were not. The trucking mafia in Quetta and Chaman, frustrated by the belligerent warlords around Kandahar who prevented expansion of their traditional goods-smuggling into Afghanistan to Iran and Central Asia, turned to the Taliban. Drawn from both Pakistani and Afghan Pashtuns, this mafia began to fund the Taliban. Soon its "customs duty" became the major source of Taliban income. As the Taliban expanded its control in Afghanistan and took over Kandahar, the

---

[2] This section relies heavily on Ahmed Rashid, "Pakistan and the Taliban," in William Maley, ed., *Fundamentalism Reborn: Afghanistan and the Taliban*, New York: New York University Press, 1998.

[3] During this same period, Pakistan's Inter-Services Intelligence Directorate (ISI), the United States, and some Arab states were supporting Ghilzai Pashtuns from central and northeastern Afghanistan.

[4] Rashid, "Pakistan," pp. 74–75.

smuggling activity grew to include Iran, Turkmenistan, and beyond into Central Asia. Soon this expanded transport system became the preferred route for heroin smugglers who contributed to Taliban coffers.[5] It is worth noting that Northern Alliance forces also engaged in the drug trade.

Viewing the unstoppable Taliban advance in 1994–1995 and desiring a secure transportation corridor for goods, and potentially energy, to and from Central Asia, the Bhutto government reversed Pakistan's support of a Pashtun government in Kabul in favor of encouraging a broadly based government that could ensure the security of a transportation corridor (both land and energy pipelines) from Peshawar to Tashkent. Its effort in 1996 to forge an alliance among Gulbuddin Hekmatyar (Pashtun), General Abdurashid Dostum (an ethnic Uzbek and former commander in the Soviet Afghan Army), and the Taliban failed. Thus, the ISI and the army pushed for closer ties to the Taliban as the government of then-President Rabbani in Afghanistan became closer to Pakistan's rivals India, Iran, and Russia.[6]

Through a combination of religious, criminal/commercial, and political interests, Pakistan became deeply involved in supporting the Taliban. In Northwest Frontier province and Baluchistan, much of Pakistan's population is ethnic Pashtun. In addition, its strategic interests in creating an Afghanistan space for its strategy of defense in depth against India argued for supporting anyone in Kabul who could provide an Afghanistan stable enough to advance that goal.

Saudi Arabian Influence

Saudi Arabia paralleled Pakistan's path of fits and starts toward support of the Taliban. Like the United States, the Saudis were strong financial backers of the mujahidin groups between 1980 and 1990.

---

[5] Ibid., pp. 77–78.

[6] Ibid., pp. 79–89.

This continued with support for Afghan Sunni elements following the mujahidin takeover in Kabul. The Saudis sought to expand neo-Wahabbism to counter growing Iranian influence (discussed in the next section) among Hazara elements among the mujahidin. Thus, the Saudis turned to the Taliban to shore up their influence in Afghanistan. Activities ranging from JUI-organized bustard-hunting trips for Saudi princes to Saudi company involvement in potential gas pipeline projects transiting Afghanistan added to the desire of the Saudi Ulema (Islamic clergy) to support the Taliban. Once the Saudi leadership was strongly committed on both a personal and a religious level, not even Taliban support for Saudi dissidents, including Osama bin Laden, could preclude Saudi engagement with the Taliban.[7]

Other Regional Powers

Situated on the western edge of the Himalayan chain and being the meeting point of Persia, Central Asia, and the subcontinent, Afghanistan has been an object of the ambitions of regional powers for centuries. It was a large part of the field where the "Great Game" between 19th century rivals Britain and Russia was played. Pakistan's regional interests have been described above. Iran, India, China, and the countries of Central Asia all have political, ethnic, economic, and strategic interests in Afghanistan. Iran and the Central Asian states play particularly significant roles.

Iranian Opposition to the Taliban

Iran's Islamic Revolution further whetted the country's already significant political, cultural, and strategic interests in Afghanistan—and challenged Saudi Arabia's leadership among the anti-Soviet Afghan forces. Distracted by the Iran-Iraq war and internal power struggles in Teheran, Iran was forced to limit its role in Afghanistan between 1980 and 1988. With clerical domination in Teheran, Iranian sup-

---

[7] Rashid, *Taliban*.

port of radical, pro-Iran, Afghan Shiite elements increased, thus offending both Pakistan and Saudi Arabia.

After the Ayatollah Khomeini's death in 1989, Teheran shifted to a foreign policy focused on state and Persian nationalist interests, including now Central Asia as well as Afghanistan. This changed Iran's focus from promoting strictly Afghan Shiite interests to a broader effort directed at Persian-speaking Sunni Afghans as well. The resulting anti-Pashtun Northern Alliance gave Iran a role in Afghanistan that it had lacked up to this point. This was not without cost. Tajik commander Ahmad Massoud turned on his Iranian supporters to once again receive Western backing, causing Iran to shift its support to Hekmatyar, whom Saudi Arabia and Pakistan also backed.

As the Taliban emerged, Iran faced an anti-Shia, anti-Iranian challenge to its interests in Afghanistan. In turn, Teheran solidified its support for Rabbani, Massoud (again), and Ismail Khan (in the process, creating an informal alliance with India and Russia) to oppose the Taliban, which controlled the vast majority of the country. Teheran believed that the rise of the Taliban was the result of an unholy alliance of the United States, Saudi Arabia, and Pakistan. This was reinforced by the U.S. and Saudi common interest in developing a gas pipeline from the Caspian region through Afghanistan to Pakistan.

The Taliban takeover in Kabul was a major blow to Iran's objectives. Iran refused to recognize the new government and continued its support of Massoud and Dostum. It also continued to be concerned about the U.S. role in Afghanistan, which it saw as part of a broader U.S. strategy to surround and block Iranian influence in the region.[8]

Central Asia's Divergent Interests

As they struggled with their own internal challenges following the breakup of the Soviet Union, leaders of the new Central Asian states were particularly concerned about the civil war in Tajikistan and the

---

[8] Ahady, pp. 118–134.

ongoing conflict in Afghanistan and how these affected their relationships with Russia. With ethnic compatriots (e.g., Uzbek and Tajik) contending for power in Afghanistan and emerging economic interests, in particular trade and possible oil and gas pipelines, developments in Afghanistan became critical challenges for these new states. Meanwhile, Russia sought to manipulate security discussions within the Commonwealth of Independent States (CIS) to reinforce Russian concerns about the emergence of the Taliban as a threat requiring collective (but Russian-led) military action.

Turkmenistan avoided taking an explicitly anti-Taliban stance, conscious of the need to protect its interests in the hope of an eventual gas pipeline route from Turkmenistan through Afghanistan. Turkmenistan stopped short of recognizing the Taliban regime, but it did develop some trade ties and dialogue with its neighbor.

Uzbekistan had its own strategic objectives in Afghanistan. Ethnic Uzbeks represented one of the major groups of the Northern Alliance. Members of the Islamic Movement of Uzbekistan (IMU), which aimed to replace Uzbekistan's secular government with an Islamic one as the first step toward a global caliphate, were receiving training in Afghanistan. The group had close ties with Pakistan's ISI, al Qaeda, and, by extension, the Taliban. In the period immediately before September 11, 2001, however, Uzbekistan had taken some steps toward détente with the Taliban, consisting of highly unofficial overtures and contacts. This may have been spurred in large part by the hope that such contacts might lead to an end to Taliban and al Qaeda support of the IMU, which was staging regular incursions into Uzbekistan and Kyrgyzstan, some of them from bases in Tajikistan.

The Taliban had also supported factions in Tajikistan's civil war, and ethnic Tajiks represented another major Northern Alliance component. The two civil wars were, in fact, deeply intertwined, and after Tajikistan's war concluded, its fledgling government was particularly keen to prevent additional conflict spillover from Afghanistan. Militarily, economically, and politically weak, however, the government had (and has) little control outside the capital city, and it was dependent on Russia for military support. Russian troops patrolled its border with Afghanistan.

Although Russia and the Central Asian states did not have a common position on Afghanistan, there were shared concerns on the part of Russia, Uzbekistan, and Tajikistan which led to a measure of coordination and cooperation in supporting the Northern Alliance. At the same time, as the Taliban appeared to cement its position, its neighbors, starting with Turkmenistan, began to think that if the regime was there to stay, perhaps it made sense to develop a *modus vivendi* with it, however unappealing this might be.

Global Powers

The United States and the Soviet Union

In addition to the competition among regional powers for influence in pre-9/11 Afghanistan, larger powers battling for global influence also played a role. Throughout the 1980s, Afghanistan was a proxy location for superpower confrontation. In the end, the Soviet Union lost the military phase of the Afghanistan conflict and the United States lost interest. U.S. military assistance to the mujahidin ended in 1991, and economic assistance ended in 1993. As the Taliban moved closer to power in 1996, U.S. diplomacy became more active.

The United States sought to engage the new Taliban authorities in Afghanistan at some level short of recognition. One motivating factor was the potential role of Afghanistan as a transport corridor for Caspian energy resources. In addition, there was hope that the Taliban would be able to deliver a peaceful and stable Afghanistan after a decade and a half of strife and that it could suppress the Afghan drug trade. Whatever the motivation, the U.S. activism clearly placed the United States with Saudi Arabia and Pakistan against India, Iran, and Russia regarding support for the Taliban. From the Taliban's perspective, USG support for the energy company Unocal carried with it the promise of U.S. diplomatic recognition.[9]

---

[9] Rashid, *Taliban*, pp. 161–167.

As fighting continued in Afghanistan and the commercial aspects of a gas pipeline through that country became more doubtful, enthusiasm for the project waned, both among corporate interests and inside the U.S. government. At the same time, more public attention was being focused on the Taliban's treatment of Afghan women. It was soon clear that the United States was not seriously considering any moves toward recognition of the Taliban regime. This perception was confirmed when the United States bombed Osama bin Laden's camps in Afghanistan in 1998.[10]

Following the dissolution of the Soviet Union in late 1991, Russia behaved more like a regional power than a superpower. Rather than pursuing its engagement as part of an aggressive global agenda, Moscow approached Afghanistan from a defensive posture aimed at preventing the spread of radical Islam into Central Asia and Russia itself. With the rise of the Taliban, containing its influence inside Afghanistan became an explicit goal. In working (with Uzbekistan and Tajikistan) to funnel arms and supplies to the Northern Alliance, Russia aligned its interests with those of India and Iran. At the same time, however, the Russians were seeking to block U.S. inroads into Central Asia and Afghanistan, in particular Washington's support for non-Russian pipeline options for Caspian energy resources.[11] Obviously, an important subtext in all of this was Moscow's humiliating retreat from Afghanistan in 1989.

The UN Role in Afghanistan

In this morass of pre-9/11 internal conflict and external intervention, the United Nations sought to facilitate a political solution to what had become a decades-long armed conflict and to provide a coordinating role for delivering humanitarian assistance to Afghanistan. UN peacemaking efforts stumbled from the beginning. The initial engagement occurred in connection with the April 1988 Geneva Accords that involved Afghanistan and Pakistan as parties to the

---

[10] Ibid., pp. 170–175.

[11] Marsden, pp. 136–137.

Accords and the United States and the Soviet Union as witnesses/guarantors. Following the Soviet withdrawal in February 1989, the Office of the Secretary General in Afghanistan and Pakistan (OSGAP) sought to create an interim government in Afghanistan. This effort, which attempted to include at least some of the Afghan resistance groups and key commanders in Afghanistan as well as the government, collapsed when the communist Najibullah regime fell in April 1992. In December 1993, the UN General Assembly established a Special Mission to Afghanistan. This period was marked by a major elevation in the status accorded by the United Nations to some of the resistance groups, undercutting the position of the government in Kabul. Finally, in May 1996, the appointment of a new head of the Special Mission coincided with the rise of the Taliban as a force in the internal political mix. The Taliban displayed little interest in negotiating with anyone—the United Nations or the other Afghan groups—believing that it could achieve its objectives through military force.[12]

The United Nations' peacemaking efforts sought an alternative to the existing political arrangements. The efforts were blocked on one hand by the unwillingness of Kabul government authorities to agree to their own demise and on the other by the ambitions of leaders of resistance groups unwilling to give power to any "transitional authority" that excluded them. The United Nations' credibility was undercut when it gave protection to Najibullah in the UN headquarters in Kabul. By the time Najibullah was murdered in the UN compound, many Afghans saw the United Nations as an accomplice of his and a participant in the human rights abuses he had committed while leading the Afghan government and, earlier, as head of the Afghan secret police, the KHAD. Further, there was unwillingness by UN mediators to address the misbehavior of UN member states, including Pakistan.[13] At one point or another, all parties—internal and

---

[12] William Maley, "The UN and Afghanistan: 'Doing Its Best' or 'Failure of a Mission'?" in William Maley, ed., *Fundamentalism Reborn: Afghanistan and the Taliban*, New York: New York University Press, 1998, pp. 186–187.

[13] Ibid., pp. 193–194.

external—had reason to question whether the United Nations could provide a political solution.

This questioning of the United Nations' ability to mediate the political conflict inside Afghanistan affected perceptions of its humanitarian and developmental assistance activities. Indeed, at an early stage, UN assistance specialists took pains to distinguish their activities from those of the UN political mediators. A further separation occurred when the United Nations divided the humanitarian and economic-development roles. That only weakened the organization's agenda in Afghanistan, where an integrated approach to the political and economic context of the conflict was required. In addition, the inability of the UN system, with its independent specialized and technical agencies, each answerable to its own governing board, to act in a collective, coherent manner reinforced the image of the organization as an incoherent and (at times) counterproductive actor. UN agencies provided humanitarian assistance to refugees in Pakistan and Iran and development assistance through Kabul. All of this, in principle, was done through the United Nations Office for the Coordination of Humanitarian and Economic Assistance Programs (UNOCA) relating to Afghanistan, which was headquartered in Geneva. Many of the independent UN agencies (e.g., UNDP, UNHCR), however, saw UNOCA as a competitor and an unnecessary departure from the traditional lead-agency approach. UNDP, operating from Kabul, in particular resisted UNOCA's coordination, while agencies operating from Pakistan and Iran were more receptive. Still, UNOCA (and later UNOCHA) was able to create and maintain a certain humanitarian space where assistance could be provided to populations throughout the country, regardless of which faction was in control.[14]

By 1997, however, the United Nations' Administrative Committee on Coordination was pressing for an integrated strategy that put assistance to Afghanistan in a geopolitical and economic context, with agreement on priorities, a single funding mechanism, and consistent implementation of human rights principles (especially con-

---

[14] Donini, pp. 26–31.

cerning the treatment of women).[15] By that time, with the Taliban in control of Afghanistan, it was too late to make up for lost opportunities with this new strategic approach.

Opium and Counternarcotics Efforts

Afghanistan's major opium production continued to concern Washington. Cultivation of opium poppies took place in both Taliban and Northern Alliance–controlled areas, and Afghanistan remained a major source of opiates for Europe and, to a lesser extent, the United States, accounting for an estimated 72 percent of global illicit opium output in 2000, according to the State Department.[16] The United States tried to address this problem through the "Six Plus Two Group" (six neighbors—Iran, Pakistan, China, Tajikistan, Uzbekistan, and Turkmenistan—plus the United States and Russia), which convened periodically to address issues pertaining to Afghanistan.[17] This group, minus Turkmenistan, signed a Regional Action Plan to address the problem in September. 2000. As a major donor, the United States also actively supported the United Nations Drug Control Program (UNDCP) in its efforts to promote alternative crops and the eradication of opium poppy cultivation.[18]

American response to the Taliban anti-drug effort prior to September 11 reflected considerable uncertainty with respect to the effort's seriousness and impact. In March 2001, President Bush refused to certify Afghanistan (along with Burma) as cooperative in counterdrug efforts. He noted a Taliban ban on poppy cultivation but said that such a ban might not have any discernible effect on sup-

---

[15] Keating, pp. 136–144.

[16] U.S. Department of State, *International Narcotics Control Strategy Report 2000*, especially the section on Southwest Asia. The report is available at http://www.state.gov/g/inl/rls/nrcrpt/2000/.

[17] Ibid.

[18] U.S. Department of State, "Transcript: U.S. Officials on Humanitarian Aid to Afghanistan," May 23, 2001.

ply, due to stockpiles.[19] Then, in May, Alan Eastham, the Acting Assistant Secretary of State for South Asia, assessed the Taliban's efforts favorably.[20] In August, Assistant Secretary of State for South Asia Christine Rocca pledged $1.5 million to support the UNDCP's assistance to former poppy farmers to promote foodstuff agriculture in Taliban-controlled areas.[21] But the Drug Enforcement Agency's October 2001 assessment of the Taliban's overall efforts toward drug control was profoundly negative, noting in particular that prices for opium had not increased in the target markets of Europe and the United States because stockpiling allowed the supply of opium to be largely independent of current production.[22]

---

[19] U.S. Department of State, "Statement of Explanation for Afghan Drug Non-Certification," March 2, 2001.

[20] U.S. Department of State, "Transcript: U.S. Officials on Humanitarian Aid to Afghanistan."

[21] U.S. Department of State, "Rocca on $1.5 Million to Aid Former Afghan Poppy Growers," August 2, 2001, available at http://www.usembassy.it/file2001_08/alia/a1080204.htm.

[22] U.S. Department of State, "DEA Administrator Testifies on Taliban and Drug Trafficking," October 3, 2001, available at http://www.usembassy.it/file2001_10/alia/a1100315.htm.

References

"Afghanistan: Humanitarian Liaison Centre Opens in Islamabad," UNOCHA Integrated Regional Information Network, December 4, 2001.

Ahady, Anwar-ul-Haq, "Saudi Arabia, Iran and the Conflict in Afghanistan," in William Maley, ed., *Fundamentalism Reborn: Afghanistan and the Taliban*, New York: New York University Press, 1998.

Bensahel, Nora, "Humanitarian Relief and Nation Building in Somalia," in Robert J. Art and Patrick Cronin, eds., *The United States and Coercive Diplomacy After the Cold War*, Washington, DC: United States Institute of Peace Press, 2003.

Bowden, Mark, *Black Hawk Down: A Story of Modern War*, New York: Atlantic Monthly Press, 1999.

Brooke, James, "Pentagon Tells Troops in Afghanistan: Shape Up and Dress Right," *New York Times*, September 12, 2002.

Brooke, James, "U.S. Tasks in Afghan Desert: Hunt Taliban, Tote Plywood," *New York Times*, September 14, 2002.

Clark, Kate, "Afghans Are the World's Most Displaced People," BBC News, April 24, 2001.

The Clinton Administration's Policy on Managing Complex Contingency Operations: Presidential Decision Directive May 1997, PDD-56 White Paper.

"Crisis in Afghanistan," Oxfam Update Humanitarian Situation, January 11, 2002.

Department of the Army, *FM 41-10: Civil Affairs Operations*, Washington, DC: Headquarters, Department of the Army, 2000.

de Torrente, Nicholas, "The War on Terror's Challenge to Humanitarian Action," in *Humanitarian Exchange*, London: Overseas Development Institute, November 2002.

Donini, Antonio, *The Policies of Mercy: UN Coordination in Afghanistan, Mozambique, and Rwanda*, Providence, RI: The Watson Institute for International Studies, Brown University, Occasional Paper No. 22, 1996.

Elmquist, Michael, *CIMIC in East Timor—An Account of Civil-Military Cooperation, Coordination and Collaboration in the Early Phases of the East Timor Relief Operation*, Geneva: United Nations Office for the Coordination of Humanitarian Affairs, 1999.

Esposito, John, *Unholy War: Terror in the Name of Islam*, New York: Oxford University Press, 2002.

Fisk, Robert, "Return to Afghanistan: Americans Begin to Suffer Grim and Bloody Backlash," *The Independent* (London), August 14, 2002.

Garvelink, William J., USAID Senior Deputy Assistant Administrator for Democracy, Conflict, and Humanitarian Assistance, "Humanitarian Assistance Following Military Operations: Overcoming Barriers," testimony before the Committee on Government Reform, Subcommittee on National Security, Emerging Threats, and International Relations, U.S. House of Representatives, May 13, 2003.

Giordono, Joseph, "GIs Show Afghan Orphans 'We're Here to Help,'" *European Stars and Stripes*, July 12, 2002.

Hamblet, William P., and Jerry G. Kline, "Interagency Cooperation: PDD 56 and Complex Contingency Operations," *Joint Force Quarterly*, Spring 2000.

"Humanitarian Leaders Ask White House to Review Policy Allowing American Soldiers to Conduct Humanitarian Relief Programs in Civ," InterAction news release, April 2, 2002.

Keating, Michael, "Dilemmas of Humanitarian Assistance in Afghanistan," in William Maley, ed., *Fundamentalism Reborn: Afghanistan and the Taliban*, New York: New York University Press, 1998.

Lakshmanan, Indira A.R., "Boredom Is Surgical Team's Ideal Battleground Scenario," *Boston Globe*, October 6, 2002.

Maley, William, "The UN and Afghanistan: 'Doing Its Best' or 'Failure of a Mission'?" in William Maley, ed., *Fundamentalism Reborn: Afghanistan and the Taliban*, New York: New York University Press, 1998.

Marsden, Peter, *The Taliban: War, Religion and the New Order in Afghanistan*, New York: Zed Books, 1998.

Minear, Larry, Ted van Baarda, and Marc Sommers, *NATO and Humanitarian Action in the Kosovo Crisis*, Providence, RI: Thomas J. Watson Institute for International Affairs, Brown University, Occasional Paper No. 36, 2000.

Perito, Robert, "Establishing the Rule of Law in Iraq," *United States Institute of Peace Special Report 104*, April 2003.

Perusse, Roland I., *Haitian Democracy Restored, 1991–1995*, New York: University Press of America, 1995.

Pirnie, Bruce R., *Civilians and Soldiers: Achieving Better Coordination*, Santa Monica, CA: RAND Corporation, MR-1026-SRF, 1998.

Rashid, Ahmed, "Pakistan and the Taliban," in William Maley, ed., *Fundamentalism Reborn: Afghanistan and the Taliban*, New York: New York University Press, 1998.

Rashid, Ahmed, *Taliban: Militant Islam, Oil and Fundamentalism in Central Asia*, New Haven, CT: Yale University Press, 2001.

Schmitt, Eric, "In Afghanistan: What's Past and What's Still to Come," *New York Times*, October 13, 2002.

Scott, James, "Rebuilding a Country, One Village at a Time," *Charleston Post and Courier* (SC), July 14, 2002.

Seiple, Chris, *The U.S. Military/NGO Relationship in Humanitarian Interventions*, Carlisle, PA: U.S. Army War College Peacekeeping Institute, 1996.

Singleton, Barbara J., *A British Agencies Afghanistan Group Briefing Paper on the Development of Joint Regional Teams in Afghanistan*, London: Refugee Council, January 2003.

The Strategic Framework and Principled Common Programming: A Challenge to Humanitarian Assistance, Overseas Development Institute, September 4, 2001.

UNDP/UNOCHA Assistance for Afghanistan Weekly Update, Issue No. 428, September 6, 2001.

UNDP/UNOCHA Assistance for Afghanistan Weekly Update, Issue No. 429, September 12, 2001.

"UN Evacuates Afghanistan Staff," BBC News, September 12, 2001.

"UN Pulls Workers Out of South Afghanistan," BBC News Dispatches, March 24, 1998.

United Nations, "Strategic Framework for Afghanistan Endorsed by UN Agencies," January 4, 1999.

United Nations Office for the Coordination of Humanitarian Assistance to Afghanistan, "Donor Alert: To Support an Inter-Agency Emergency Humanitarian Assistance Plan for Afghans in Afghanistan and Neighboring Countries (October 2001–March 2002)," September 27, 2001.

United Nations Office for the Coordination of Humanitarian Assistance to Afghanistan, "30 Day Emergency Operational Assistance Plan for Afghanistan: 15 November–15 December 2001," November 15, 2001.

United Nations Secretary General, *Report of the Secretary General on the Humanitarian Implications of the Measures Imposed by Security Council Resolutions 1267 (1999) and 1333 (2000) on Afghanistan*, July 13, 2001.

U.S. Agency for International Development, "Afghanistan—Complex Emergency," Situation Report No. 4 (FY 2003), March 13, 2003.

"U.S. Announces Afghan Aid Package," BBC News, May 17, 2001.

U.S. Department of State, "DEA Administrator Testifies on Taliban and Drug Trafficking," October 3, 2001.

U.S. Department of State, *International Narcotics Control Strategy Report 2000*, especially the section on Southwest Asia.

U.S. Department of State, "Rocca on $1.5 Million to Aid Former Afghan Poppy Growers," August 2, 2001.

U.S. Department of State, "Statement of Explanation for Afghan Drug Non-Certification," March 2, 2001.

U.S. Department of State, "Transcript: U.S. Officials on Humanitarian Aid to Afghanistan," May 23, 2001.

"U.S. Officials on Rare Afghanistan Visit," BBC News, April 18, 2001.

"U.S. Troops Working Relief to Modify Clothing," *Washington Post*, April 21, 2002.